Whispers
of
Wisdom

From Mammography to Mastectomy –
One Woman's Journey with God

By
Barb Dunn

Whispers of Wisdom
From Mammography to Mastectomy - One Woman's Journey with God
by Barb Dunn

Printed in the United States of America

ISBN 9781498401418

Scripture quotations taken from the English Standard Version (ESV). Copyright © 2001 by Crossway, a publishing ministry of Good News Publishers. Used by permission. All rights reserved.

Scripture quotations taken from the New International Version (NIV). Copyright © 1973, 1978, 1984, 2011 by Biblica, Inc.™. Used by permission. All rights reserved.

Scripture quotations taken from the New American Standard Bible (NASB). Copyright © 1960, 1962, 1963, 1968, 1971, 1972, 1973, 1975, 1977, 1995 by The Lockman Foundation. Used by permission. All rights reserved.

www.xulonpress.com

To my husband and sons with all my love – may God's word comfort you, may His Holy Spirit guide you and may His angels protect you all the days of your life.

To the reader

I n the corner of my kitchen stands a hand-painted block with the words, "Let us be silent that we may hear the whisper of God," a quote by Ralph Waldo Emerson. It touches my heart and reminds me that if I am still and quietly listen for God's word, he will whisper words of comfort and guidance to me. God is in my life always, but never more than on difficult days when I am faced with complicated and frightening situations. God's word is powerful. When He whispers into my heart, He quells my fears, instills in me an inner peace and strength, and enlightens me to make the right decisions. I encourage you to invite God to be part of your everyday life and your decision-making as well. God wants to hear from us and He wants us to hear from Him too.

Table of Contents

Introduction

This book is a series of reflections related to my faith and my journey which led me to a bilateral mastectomy in March of 2012. The intent of this book is not to be a medical guide to manage breast cancer and it may not include every option that is available to women. There are many valuable resources available to serve that purpose. I do, however, try to share as much medical and technical information about my situation as possible. I must stress the importance of always seeking professional care and praying before making any major decisions about your health. You must feel peace about each course of action you take and do what is appropriate and best for you.

I was diagnosed as high risk with atypical lobular hyperplasia (ALH) in both breasts. Decisions regarding the treatments that were available to me may seem negotiable in some ways. All the more reason to stress that my journey was one with God and what I felt He wanted me to do. I believe my daily devotion to our Lord was the best part of my journey and the foundation for my peace and direction.

It is my hope that as you read my story you have a sense of my heart, my humanness and strength, as well as my vulnerability. I also pray that the verses shared will inspire you to read the bible. God's word is fluid and alive. It tells of the past, speaks to you in the present and gives you the promise of a future. For that, I am eternally grateful. To Him, Be the Glory!

Chapter 1

Take Everything
To Him In Prayer

J anuary 9, 2011: I find a small lump. It feels like one of
those mini chocolate eggs that I can't seem to get enough
of during the Easter season. Resting in the upper quadrant of
my left breast, we are introduced to each other quite by accident, my hand brushing over it as I roll over in bed in a drowsy
state. Yet this seemingly insignificant action sets off a firestorm
of emotions in me.

Now fully awake, I lie in bed terrified and think, "What
is this?" "Where did it come from?" "How long has it been
there?" I send up a quick prayer to God, not sure what to ask
for but knowing I need Him. Sleep continues to elude me, as

I lay on my back in the darkness, eyes wide-open, wishing I could take back these last few minutes. I try to focus on my husband's steady, even breathing, hoping it will lull me to sleep. In only a few hours he will awake for his predawn trek to work. I try not to wake him as I wrestle with my feelings. I am torn between never wanting to know what this is and the need to know immediately – but somehow I already know.

The alarm rings at 4 a.m. and Dan, my husband and soul mate of more than twenty years, gets up and starts to get ready for work. I lay in bed waiting to steal his attention before he leaves for the day. I have an uneasy feeling which I want to chalk up to a bad dream, but I know it's a harbinger of things to come. Before heading out the bedroom door, Dan kisses me goodbye, but today I hastily grab his hand to stop him. "Feel this," I say, "Have you ever felt this before?" Hoping he will say, "I don't feel anything," I touch his beautifully rugged face and search his blue eyes for some sort of confirmation that there is nothing there and that I have indeed gone insane. Instead he calmly looks into my face and says, "No, go to the doctor." And off he goes.

I lay in bed trying to get some sleep until it's time to get the boys off to school. A buddy of John's, my eldest son, arrives at 7 a.m. to drive him to the high school. I wake up Daniel, my youngest son, prepare his breakfast and drive him to the junior high around the corner from our house. At exactly 9 a.m., I call my doctor's office and make an appointment. After performing my "mom" duties, I am now finally able to contemplate my situation over my morning coffee. As I sit at my kitchen counter, my hand instinctively goes to my left breast. It's still there, in my breast and on my mind. I cannot seem to think about anything else and I become more anxious. I feel an immediate, intense need to reach out to my friends and so I quickly dash off an email to my Yadas.

Suzanne, Courtney and Linda – or my Yadas as I have dubbed them – are my dear bible study friends and my "go-to" prayer warriors who help provide direction and guidance in my life. There is something so empowering about having friends who you can call on to pray for you. (My thanks to Neta Jackson, author of The Yada Yada Prayer Group series, who inspired four friends to form an interpersonal bond and an equally devoted prayer group.) We love each other. We care for each other. We pray for each other. We are the Yadas!

If you do not have friends who you can call on for prayer, get some! Below are some of the personal communications my Yadas exchanged, and God's word they shared with me.

January 10, 2011 – 9:15 a.m.

My email to Suzanne, Courtney and Linda:

Hey my Yadas! Please pray for me to stop these anxious thoughts. I found a ping-pong in my left breast last night. Going to get it checked out tomorrow. Already planning my memorial service. Either that or what size replacements I want!

Suzanne's response via text:

Got it babe. Praying!

Courtney's response via email:

Barb, I pray for the Lord to take all anxieties away – to fill you with His presence and to hold you tight in His arms. I pray for His comfort and assurance to you. He will carry you through the exam and you know that His plans are in charge. He will always be faithful to you and give you all your prayer requests as you pray through your heart to Him.

Linda's response via email:

Okay Barb … what the heck size is a ping-pong? Glad you were able to get an appointment so soon. What time is your appointment tomorrow? I am praying and will continue to pray throughout your appointment. I will admit … I did laugh about the size of replacements. Remember, 1 John 4:4: He who is in you is greater than he who is in the world. He will give you a peace that only He can give.

Psalm 94:19—When my anxious thoughts multiply within me, your consolations delight my soul.

Psalm 32:7—You are my hiding place, you preserve me from trouble; You surround me with songs of deliverance. Keep singing those praise songs Barb!

Psalm 55:22—Cast your burden upon the Lord and He will sustain you; He will never allow the righteous to be shaken.

Psalm 56: 3 and 4—When I am afraid, I will put my trust in You. In God whose word I praise; In God I have put my trust, I shall not be afraid.

Lamentations 3:22-24—The Lord's loving kindnesses indeed never cease, for His compassions never fail. They are new every morning; great is your faithfulness. The Lord is my portion, says my soul, therefore I have hope in Him.

*Hang in there babe ... the Yadas are with you
every step of the way.*

I print and tuck the response from Linda into my bible and refer to these verses many times. My prayers, those of my friends and God's word are not only appropriate, but also essential to my journey in life, to my decisions, to my every moment. As I begin my journey, I feel the need to enlist an army of prayer warriors and I am encouraged and grateful to know I am in their prayers. I also know that God's word will steady me and guide me along the way.

In my opinion, this is the foundation for everything: consult God's word and pray, and ask others to pray for you with strength and purpose. There is something so uplifting about praying and knowing others are praying for you. For several years I have kept a prayer journal, adding meaningful scripture when I need a quick reference to God's word. It helps to write down my thoughts and feelings as it enables me to better focus on others' needs. I continue to challenge myself and add to the journal the names and requests of those who ask for prayer.

At times it can be overwhelming, but I know God hears every request and when I reflect on past entries, I am in awe of how He handles the needs of others.

Chapter 2

He Is With Me

My visit to the doctor yields a mammography script and a cautionary, "Don't jump to any conclusions." Anxiously, I email more prayer requests to my dear friends. Throughout the day, I silently quote one of my favorite verses from *Philippians 4:6: Do not be anxious about anything, but in everything, pray.* I am an anxious person by nature, but this verse helps ground me in the truth that God is in control and anxiety is not a productive emotion.

Part of my anxiety stems from the fact that I know too much. They say knowledge is power and it is, if it empowers you, but does not overpower you. I have taught classes about multiple disease states and various medicines, and at one time even worked in a clinical laboratory. Having a medical background and more than twenty years experience in the healthcare and pharmaceutical industries has prepared me mentally, but not emotionally. Intellectually, I am able to understand the possibilities and the options awaiting me, but I can't stop my mind as it runs miles ahead of me, taking me down a path I don't want to go.

I manage to get through most of the day, but later as I drive to the local rink to watch my son John play ice hockey, I am isolated with my thoughts. Into the winter's darkness on solitary back roads, I feel very alone and my mind wanders back to the lump. I begin to think the worst. Suddenly, tears start to roll down my face, the salty drops moistening my cheeks. The radio is tuned to my favorite contemporary Christian radio station. I turn my focus to the song playing and begin to softly sing along, willing the message to resonate. As the tune emanates from the radio, it seems to be playing just for me. The Afters are singing the song, "Light Up the Sky" and the lyrics speak straight to my heart – "You light up the sky to show me that you are with me." Yes! He is with me! In that moment of feeling alone, God reminds me of the simple yet most beautiful fact of my life. I am never alone for He is with me always. What makes it even more significant is that I come to this realization during one of my favorite times of day. There are few things that bring me more joy in life than to look up into the dark evening sky saturated with twinkling stars and revel in His majestic creation saying, "God I love You!"

On this black night, my God, the creator of the universe, sees me and gives me a very special message. He reminds me that He is with me always and I feel it in my heart.

God tells me this because I am special and unique to Him. So are you! I encourage you to really think about this. God loves you as He loves me. He died for you and yearns to have a relationship with you now as you walk through life and for all eternity. God the Almighty is an awesome God, but He is not so big that He is not involved in the details of our lives. His presence is constant, even though there are times in our busy lives when we don't acknowledge Him or listen long enough to hear what He is saying. Anytime I feel alone, I remind myself of the message I heard that dark night. He is with me! I hope you remember that God is with you also. Invite Him into your heart and journey with Him in your life. Life can be daunting, even frightening, but God is our constant companion and guide if we allow Him to lead.

> *So do not fear, for I am with you; do not be dismayed, for I am your God. I will strengthen you and help you. Isaiah 41:10 ESV*

Chapter 3

Nothing Is Too Complicated For God

Three days later ... and so it begins. Today I go to the Women's Breast Center to get the dreaded mammogram. I get John and Daniel off to school, straighten the house and wait, prescription in hand, for Renee to arrive. Renee is my mother-in-law (I call her Mom) and all-around saint. A retired neonatal intensive care and operating room nurse, there is no talking Mom out of coming with me. As soon as the car arrives, I get in and Mom begins talking about our upcoming trip to Costco, doing her best to distract me from my current situation and destination.

At the breast center, Mom sits by my side as I fill out the registration forms. She continues to stay with me as we move into the waiting area – my moral support before going into an exam room. I look around at the women sitting near me, and wonder why they are there and say a little prayer for their outcomes. Finally, I am escorted down a long corridor and into an exam room where I see what I believe to be the same machine used for torture during medieval times.

I know the routine well. I started getting mammograms at age forty, as per the recommendation of the American Cancer Society. Thankfully, all have been negative thus far. Although I acknowledge that regular mammograms are extremely important since early detection of breast cancer can save lives, I don't look forward to having my breasts tugged and pulled and then, finally, squished flat until they resemble pancakes. (Does any woman?)

The torture begins. Two rounds of pictures plus two sets of ultrasounds. They even add in the right breast. I guess I should be thankful for the thoroughness of it all. The technician tells me the mammography is complete, but asks me to wait in the exam room.

After a few minutes, which seem like hours, a radiologist, patient navigator and technician come in. "Oh boy! This cannot be good," I think to myself. I remain sitting on the exam table but my feet want to run out of there as fast as they can. The technician sheepishly stands by the wall while the patient navigator sits with a clipboard, ready to take notes. The radiologist (the only one without breasts) starts to speak. "Your breasts are complicated," he says. I can tell complicated is not good by the look on their faces. "Seriously?" I respond. "I have to tell ya doc, you're the first one to ever describe these babies as complicated! I think they're pretty straightforward!" Using humor to deal with stress has always been my coping mechanism and now I count on it to slow my rapidly beating heart, but no one laughs, including me.

Apparently like a bad weather map, the mammogram predicts I have the perfect storm brewing – cysts, calcifications and dense breasts. (Not to mention a history of hormonal cancers on both sides of my family.) The radiologist continues to talk, but I don't remember what else is said for my mind is already wandering, taking me to dark and frightening places. I picture friends and family at my funeral consoling Dan and the boys, saying how sorry they are to hear that I lost my fight against breast cancer. I snap back to reality just as the radiologist finishes speaking. Collecting myself, I walk out of the office holding pamphlets about genetic counseling, a tentative date for biopsies, phone numbers of breast surgeons and a list of oncologists, "just in case."

Mom drops me off at home after listening to me run through every possible course of action I can take. I walk into the kitchen, sit dejectedly at the counter and start to sift through all the paperwork. Trying to determine which surgeons are in my insurance plan, I am overwhelmed with whom to call first. Eventually I make the decision to just focus on the best care I can possibly get and not allow whether the surgeon is in or out of my insurance network to affect my choice. Although finances are a concern, I decide my health comes first and I must go to the surgeon I think is best.

After a few phone calls to breast surgeons, I choose one. Actually, I just decide on a receptionist because I like her so much from our phone conversation that I feel her personality is indicative of the entire office. I feel she is someone I can talk to and I am comfortable with her. She patiently listens as I explain to her the results of the mammography, the advice from the breast center team and the concerns I have about insurance and potential future needs and costs. We arrange an appointment for the following Tuesday.

The appointment with the breast surgeon is surreal in some ways, but she is an angel. A breast cancer survivor herself, I am taken in by how jovial and bright she is. I also like the way her nurse and her office manager make me feel as if we are friends and they're just welcoming me in for a cup of coffee or a girly chat instead of to discuss breast cancer. I know I am in the right place – regardless of her not being in my insurance plan.

Once alone with the doctor, she asks about my family. I proudly ramble on about my two wonderful boys and my terrific husband and tell her a little about my job. As I talk, I find myself getting more upset at the thought of leaving my life and everyone I love behind. I start to cry. Gently she hugs me and tells me she knows how I feel. And I know she does. She examines me and then refers to the black and white images of my breasts hanging on the light board. My films show calcifications, which could possibly be an indication of cancer. She concludes I need four biopsies – three stereotactic biopsies and a fine-needle aspiration in order to confirm what these aberrations suggest.

The doctor and I talk about my family history as well. I tell her that my two maternal aunts both died of hormonal cancers – uterine and metastatic breast cancer. My mother, who I still miss terribly, died almost six years ago, the only one of her sisters that did not die of cancer. I mention that my dad has prostate cancer and his mom died at forty of what they referred to back in the day as "female cancer." She says it sounds as if she may have had ovarian cancer and for the first time someone has actually put a name to her disease. The only surviving relative to have information on my grandmother, Caroline, is my dad but he was fifteen months old when his mother died.

My grandmother, Caroline, has always been near and dear to my heart as a mother who never got to raise her son. Seventy-five years earlier, when she was diagnosed, medicine did not have the resources, studies, equipment or experience to deal with her cancer. She did not have choices. I do and for that I am grateful.

Although the thought of having potentially cancerous cells in my breasts frightens me, I have information. I don't know what final decisions I will eventually make using this information, but at least I have the knowledge. Now I need the wisdom.

There are so many details, so many pieces to put together. Even with my scientific and medical background, it all seems overly complicated to me – but not to God. Nothing is too complicated for Him! I need to remember that and to remind myself to take one step at a time.

> *For nothing will be impossible with God.*
> *Luke 1:37 ESV*

On the way out, I spot a hospital magazine and take one. While waiting for the elevator, I flip through the pages, perusing the articles. One article features the breast center and some of the dedicated women who work there. I learn many are survivors of breast cancer themselves. They share their personal stories and their drive to care for and empathize with their patients. There is a picture with all of them wearing pink boxing gloves. I like that. It awakens a sense of fight in me as I get ready to prepare for battle.

Chapter 4

Trust Him No Matter What

W e do not always understand God's timing or see it as ideal. But it is actually perfect; just not always evident to us. As God's children, He gives us what is best for us at a time when it is best for us. Not privileged to pull back the curtain to see the whole story just yet, we just need to trust in Him.

During the last ten years I have been attending bible studies for women at my church. It is made up of a diverse group from the community who meet weekly for a few hours to sing praise songs, pray together and discuss different topics, usually focusing on a particular book in the bible. In addition to being a member, I sometimes lead small groups. This spring

I join a group reading the book, "The Bible Jesus Read," by Philip Yancey, led by my dear friend and mentor, Elaine. The two most compelling chapters to me are Psalms and the Book of Job.

In a chapter devoted to understanding the Psalms, Yancey says this book of the bible needs to be read as if we are looking over the shoulder of someone writing a journal. The psalmists share a rollercoaster of emotions, raw with questions and frustrations, and at the same time stand in awe and praise of God. This is exactly what I am going through. I am trusting God, seeking His advice and calling out to Him for mercy, yet at the same time I am overwhelmed with fear and the thought that I may die. In addition to my own personal fears, my heart needs to give over to God my deep concerns for my husband and sons. I am concerned about their faith, their fears and their care if something should happen to me. Yancey challenges us to write our own psalm. I am not sure I can do it, but one night, deep in thought and prayer, I find it cathartic to put my feelings on paper.

Why have I entertained darkness when You are my light?

Why do I fear when You are my Savior?

How do I do Your will when I am hesitant to go to places I do not choose?

Oh, how this world confuses me!

I want to be Your servant.

How am I doing?

I love those You blessed me with, but You love them more!

Please hold them in Your hand.

May You keep me strong and faithful for those who love me.

May they draw near to You.

I bargain with You as I consider,

If harm shall befall us, let it be me so that You may keep them from harm.

I thank You for Your saints who You gather around me.

You find ways to show me and tell me that You are here.

I hear You, my Shepard!

I know Your voice.

You make my heart be filled with joy!

You dispel my fear.

Make me bold, Lord,

My faith is in You.

You are good, loving and true.

Your light is in me.

You drive out the darkness of my mind.

My heart leaps with joy that You are with me and mine all the days of our lives.

You are my sustainer, my healer, my provider.

May I remember Your blessings and rest in Your faithfulness.

Barb Dunn–Personal Psalm of Lamentation, January 2011

A few chapters later the group reads about the Book of Job. It is the story of a human who is beset by misfortune and suffering. Initially, when I think of Job, I think of him as "the poor guy who lost everything" or "the guy with all the patience." I am afraid to be Job for he suffered so much. I think of what might happen if things don't go the way I want. It is relatively easy to trust in God and believe He's in charge when things are going our way and the world around us makes sense. But what about when things turn upside down and inside out? It is in the midst of such chaos and anguish that faith in God is needed most. I know God loves me and this is not punishment or the consequence of my own sin. I trust God and will hold onto Him no matter how my life turns out.

Two nights before my next appointment at the breast center for the biopsies, I sit at the kitchen table with my evening cup of tea, staring into space. Seeing me, Dan sits down next to me. In the past few weeks, we haven't talked much about what could possibly be coming our way. We have just been going through the motions of life. We pray and await the next procedure. On this particular night, Dan seems to know intuitively what I am thinking. He takes my hand and his words are exactly what I need to hear, "You know, no matter what this is, we are going to get through it together."

Now anyone who knows my husband knows he is not a verbose man. (I'm the talker, er, the "communicator" in the family.) Dan didn't even say the words "Will you marry me?" on the night of our engagement! Of course this has been a long-standing joke between us for our twenty plus years together. I still tease him about it, and his pat response is always, "Why else would I hand you a diamond ring?"

Over the years I have come to realize that what my husband does say is well thought out and very wise. The words he has just spoken make me feel as though someone has just injected me with all the oxygen I need to survive for the rest of my life. I am without words. All I can do is hug him and rest my tearful cheek on his broad shoulders. He says more to me through expressions of love than with mere words. No matter what, my husband loves me and his strength will be my strength. With God and my loving husband at my side, I am ready for what is ahead.

> *Trust in the Lord with all your heart; do not lean on your own understanding. In all your ways acknowledge Him and He will make straight your paths. Proverbs 3:5-6 ESV*

Chapter 5

His Will, Not Mine

It is increasingly common for a woman to need a follow-up mammogram or an additional diagnostic breast procedure at some point in her life. Clusters of calcifications and dense breasts seen on exams may be early signs of breast cancer. Newer digital imaging "sees" a lot more and doctors need to thoroughly rule out disease. If a woman does need a biopsy, there is usually a suspicion that the doctor wants to fully investigate. If I were a card player, I'd swear I just drew a "full house" of suspicion. I need one fine needle aspiration and three stereotactic biopsies! A stereotactic biopsy removes a tiny section of breast tissue and a fine-needle aspiration drains fluid from cysts or lesions in the breast. Both types of samples are then sent to pathology for further evaluation.

January 27, 2011: Dan and I get up early and head to the breast center shortly before 6 a.m. Dan's parents are on kid duty so they will soon arrive at our house to wake the boys and make sure they get off to school.

After a thirty-minute drive, Dan and I walk into the breast center and register. A nurse comes out, hands Dan a remote for the mounted television, and tells him he can sit in the waiting room. Dan kisses me and then moves to the designated room, choosing instead to settle down with a book.

This seems all too familiar, all too soon. I hang my clothes in the locker and put on the robe the center provides. It is warm and soft. Pulling it closely around me, I tie the belt and sit down, catching up on a few back issues of "People" while I wait. I hear the nurse call my name and I stand up and follow her into the ultrasound room. As I disrobe, she explains she will be performing the fine needle biopsy first. Placing some cold, sticky gel on my left breast, she starts to move a transducer over the area where the lump is located – back and forth, back and forth. She looks at the screen and, seeing the target area, informs me she has located the cyst. It looks like a black hole in the midst of squiggly, white lines running through the image of my breast on the screen. She marks it and calls in the radiologist. A friendly, slim woman, who looks all of twenty-five years old, walks in and introduces herself. She apologizes as she proceeds to insert a needle into my breast while the technician keeps the transducer in place as her guide. Slowly the needle inhales the suspicious fluid. She labels it and seals it for transport to the pathology lab for testing. The technician wipes away the small spot of blood on my chest and hands me back my robe. As the radiologist leaves, she says she will see me in the stereotactic biopsy room.

The biopsy room is crowded with machinery and a contraption into which two women in scrubs place me. They assist the radiologist in performing three stereotactic biopsies – two on my left breast and one on my right. Anyone who says that biopsies aren't that bad is lying. All are grueling for me. I lay on my stomach the whole time, my breasts hanging through the holes in the table-like structure I rest on, allowing the medical personnel in the room to perform what feels like torture. I undergo pinches, pokes and the sensation of a few mini mammograms. I hear popping sounds as each tissue sample is gathered. It feels like a jackhammer is drilling out the calcifications. After each tissue sample, they also insert a small titanium marker for future reference. I am not allowed to move much and my limbs quickly fall asleep. The topical anesthetics don't work well. There is a lot of blood, a lot of bruising and a good amount of pain. I pray, recite scripture, and replay my favorite songs in my head. I breathe deeply and can't wait for it to be over. I am, however, at peace. I do not feel alone.

Near the end of the last biopsy, the scheduling nurse comes in to meet the patient who took up the room for the day. Talk about celebrity status! I also come to realize that one of the women in scrubs is a representative from the machine's manufacturer. She walks over to me, touches my arm and says, "Bless your heart."

They wrap me up with a pseudo floral tube top and I return to my locker to get dressed. I slowly lift my arms to get my shirt on, feeling a tinge as I button my pants and slip on my shoes. The nurses and doctor have all been encouraging and kind, but I can't wait to leave. I want to go home and go back to my normal, everyday life.

As Dan drives us home I drowsily look out the car window. "What would you like to do about dinner," he asks, trying to keep things normal. I laugh. Even with a particularly stressful day, eating is still a major priority in the Dunn household! I point to a sign for an upcoming deli and say, "I could go for a pastrami sandwich." At least my stomach hasn't been affected by the day's activities.

Dan stays home with me the day after the biopsies. The following day, he needs to return to work so Mom comes over to see what she can do for me and if there is any housework to be done. She starts a wash, empties the dishwasher and walks our dog, Buddy. When she returns, she has Courtney by her side holding a crock pot full of meatballs and spaghetti for the night's dinner. Courtney and I chat awhile and then she leads me to the couch so I can lie down and rest. I am still tired and sore from the procedures and it doesn't take long for me to fall asleep. When I awake the boys are already home from school.

A week after the biopsies I receive a call from the office manager at the breast surgeon's office. She explains the doctor wants me to get an MRI to determine if there is any change in circulation in my breasts which may be an indication of cancer.

Even though the needle biopsy is benign, all three stereotactic biopsies show multiple areas of atypical lobular hyperplasia (ALH). This is good news and bad news. The good news is that it is not cancer. The bad news is that it is considered a precursor to cancer and increases my risk. I have this dreaded feeling there is more bad news to come.

I call the hospital and ask for appointment times for the MRI. The only day they have available is Thursday, the same day Dan and I have tickets to see the Broadway play, "Wicked," a gift from my sister Carolyn. I so want to go to the play, but I know I need to book the appointment. I say yes to Thursday and resolutely decide I am going out that night – no matter how I feel!

The day of the MRI, I arrive alone at the hospital toting a bag for an evening in the city. I register, fill out paperwork and wait. The nurse reviews my medical history and escorts me to the locker room to disrobe. I assure her I have no metal in my body and no piercings, just some titanium chips. As the nurse leaves, a technician arrives to insert an intravenous needle into my hand. He immediately registers the anxiety on my face and assures me it won't hurt. I hate needles in my hands, but he is gentle and does a great job minimizing my angst. He directs me into the room ahead where I see the MRI tube, all hollow and waiting to draw me in for further inspection. Another nurse enters the room and explains how I am to lie very still in the tube and warns me the procedure is noisy. They have no music to play for me so I guess I will be playing my own Top 10 in my head once again.

As I lay on my stomach, I am not sure if the table I am lying on is moving or if the tube is moving to swallow me up. Whatever it is, my body doesn't like this magnetic wonderland. I start to feel disoriented and nauseous. I breathe deeply, over and over again. The sensation stops and I start to feel a little better.

The MRI is finally over and I get dressed, sprint to my car and drive into the city. I can't wait to meet Dan and put this day behind me. Together, we have a wonderful dinner and enjoy seeing the play. We even book a hotel in the city for the evening so Dan can get to work the next day without commuting back after a late night. It is a great respite to enjoy some time together that doesn't involve doctors, waiting rooms, procedures or prescriptions.

The next day I send a few email updates to my friends. The following gives a sense of what I am experiencing during these diagnostic procedures. I try to keep it light and focus on the need to take one step at a time. At the end of the first phase of my journey (about three months), I will have had multiple mammograms, ultrasounds, biopsies and an MRI whose results prompt the doctor to want to do a lumpectomy.

Email I send after biopsy day:

January 28, 2011

Hey ladies! I know some of this might be repetitive or you have gotten bits and pieces (no pun intended!) but just wanted you to know all went well yesterday with my biopsies. I needed one aspiration and three stereotactic. They are ultrasound guided tissue removals. Usually women get one or two on average if the doctor suspects cancer. Your classic overachiever friend needed four! Dan took me and we were there most of the day. They put titanium markers in each breast for future biopsies. What do ya think? Wonder Woman?

I am sore, but doing well except I hate needing to relax. I can't use my chest muscles for two days and it is difficult for me to reach. Luckily, I did catch up on my cleaning prior. Dan is home today so maybe we will watch movies.

God was so good (as always!) and even though the position on the table was uncomfortable, to say the least, I felt like my head was resting on Jesus' chest the whole time and that kept me calm. The staff at the breast center was awesome too.

Going to rest. Results should come next week. I am good – God is with me no matter what! Love you and felt all your prayers.

Barb

This next email came the day after I actually just got finished thanking God for taking me to an Abraham moment – a moment where you don't know the future but you rest in God's promises. God is so cool!

January 29, 2011

Hi Barb,

I wanted to share with you some words I read today from Ava Pennington's book. (Our Yada sister Suzanne had given the book, "One Year Alone With God" to all of us Yadas.) They are so fitting to your present week. The page talks about having no limits on God's presence in our lives – how we are to have no boundaries with our relationship with our Lord. Ava spoke of Abraham and how he went beyond the "normal" belief and faith and stretched his spiritual world beyond his own understanding.

" ... *Abraham realized the power of El Elyon would care for him in every area of life. El Elyon is the Lord of every part of our life: spiritual, physical, mental and emotional.*"

This passage hit me so, and the Lord just brought your beautiful face to mind as I read. I wanted to share this with you. And yes, it is on page 35 in Ava's book.

I love you!

Peace,

C.

Email I sent after I receive the biopsy results:

February 3, 2011

Subject: Benign tatas

As I address this email, I just want to say how blessed I am that I have so many wonderful friends who love me and have been there to pray and support me during the past few weeks.

My results on the biopsies are benign – no cancer! Praise God! The tissue is atypical (atypical lobular hyperplasia or ALH) in addition to being "complicated." I guess we have always known I am atypical and complicated. The results do indicate that I am at a higher risk of breast cancer as atypia (abnormal) and hyperplasia (over growth) are indicators of that. I now need an MRI since it can be used for dense breasts such as mine and also because there is a suspicion the ALH may be multicentric (in more areas). Depending, I may need some more surgery. The best way I can equate this is if you think of an atypical mole that the dermatologist would remove even though it is not yet skin cancer.

I thank you again for all your prayers, help and support as you hold me up. I praise God and am grateful, truly grateful for this experience – it brought me to an "Abraham" moment where I realized I was at the brink of something unknown, but was also willing to trust God no matter what and knew full well that He is with me.

Psalm 34:4: I sought the Lord and He answered me – He delivered me from all my fears.

Proverbs 3:5-7: Trust in the Lord with all your heart and lean not on your own understanding. In all your ways, acknowledge Him and He will lead your paths straight. Do not be wise in your own

*eyes, fear the Lord and shun evil, this will bring
health to your body and nourishment to your bones.*

Love,

Barb

I send the following email after I undergo the MRI:

February 18, 2011

Subject: Change the subject!

*Aren't you tired of hearing about breasts? I am!
But seriously … based on the latest MRI, I will
need a lumpectomy to remove two areas of my
breasts (one on each side – because I like balance?)
The areas are atypical – they are associated with
calcifications, which mean the area is prolific.
Calcifications and atypia are red flags, but are not
staged cancers. For me, it is Stage 0, but active
enough that this would be the best precaution at*

this point. They say there is a chance it may turn out to be positive for cancer, but we don't need to go there yet. I need to heal from the last procedure so probably not until end of March (before our anniversary, after hockey banquet, before Easter, Daniel's confirmation ...). It is not an emergency so maybe I can wait until May. Haha!

Most importantly, please pray I heal quickly, surgery goes well, results are good and my husband is at peace in all this. I am good — my life overflows with people I love and who love me and based on prayer requests for others, this is really small potatoes (no jokes about my tatas!).

Bible verse of the day: Psalm 73:24-26: You guide me with Your counsel, and afterward You will receive me to glory. Whom have I in heaven but You? And there is nothing on earth that I desire besides You. My flesh and my heart may fail, but

God is the strength of my heart and my portion forever.

What did I learn from all these procedures? I learned that even in the most troubled times you can be sure God loves you and has an incredible future planned for you. He is still with you as always, holding you and cradling you like a parent does with a baby.

Zephaniah 3:17 ESV really spoke to me:

The Lord your God is with you, the Mighty Warrior who saves. He will take great delight in you; in His love He will no longer rebuke you, but will rejoice over you with singing.

Chapter 6

His Will Still

Since the MRI results do not allow them to rule out disease or cancer, the surgeon explains she needs to perform a lumpectomy, as it is best to remove the growths she sees. After letting this course of action sink in, I reluctantly schedule yet another procedure for Monday, April 4th, the day after my nineteenth wedding anniversary. I don't know what to expect, but feel a little bit more heaviness about this procedure since it is real surgery. I get my blood work done the week before and am cleared to go.

The night before the lumpectomy, Dan and I attend a county awards dinner for high school ice hockey players. Our son, John, receives an award as a defenseman for his high school team. We are so proud of him. We enjoy a nice dinner and the company of John's teammates and their parents. It is a wonderful night and another reminder I have so much to live for – nineteen years of being married to a wonderful man and two great sons who love me.

As we awake to the blackness of the early morning, Dan and I get ready to make what is now a routine trip to the breast center. After the staff receives us, they start with more mammograms, but these include the radiologist inserting guide wires into both breasts to mark where the surgeon will remove the tissue. The radiologist is the same one from the day I had the biopsies. She remarks how unusual it is that I am her patient again as she rarely sees the same patient after biopsy procedures. I thank God for the apparent coincidence as her presence and sweetness bring me comfort.

Wires inserted, I settle into a wheelchair and wait in the hallway area until the attendant arrives to take me to the surgical floor. The realization of it all hits me as I sit and wait. I start to cry. All of a sudden, I hear a woman say, "Barbara, don't worry, it will be okay." I don't know who she is or how she knows my name, but somehow I feel better. Sometimes a kind word from a stranger is all that is needed.

The attendant finds me, releases the brake on the wheelchair and off we go. I give a limp wave to the compassionate stranger and look at my hands as I get pushed through the caverns of the hospital elevators and halls. On the operating floor, a nurse greets me with papers for me to approve and sign, including my living will. Horrified, I realize a dreadful mistake has been made. The papers reveal I am having a partial mastectomy, not a lumpectomy. The nurse explains that it is the same thing – they are just using different terminology. I wrestle with the mastectomy word, but relenting, I sign. Dan is escorted to my bedside before they take me away for surgery. The man of few words kisses me and simply says, "Everything will be fine."

The next person I see is the anesthesiologist who resembles a sous chef with his white hat. He makes me think about food and I realize I am hungry. He injects something into the intravenous line. Before drifting into unconsciousness, I hear the release of the hospital bed brake and a deep voice say, "Here we go."

Waking up in recovery, I see Dan by my side. He gently tells me to just relax and take my time. The breast surgeon comes by and informs us all went well and she will see me in her office in a few days. Dan helps me get dressed, talks to the nurse about discharge instructions and we head home. Last month, I was wrapped tightly and was purple and bruised from getting "drilled" in multiple areas of each breast. This time I am wrapped again with stitches, gauze and a new tube top. All I can think about is removing the bandages to see the aftermath of the operation.

A few more weeks of healing and following doctor's orders. No reaching, stretching or cleaning! While most women would think receiving instructions not to clean is great, I hate the limitations. It is also a continuous reminder that my life is anything but normal. Mom remains a constant at the house, keeping things orderly, dividing her time between me, the dog, the laundry and meals for the family. My Yadas also bring dinners to the house and look in on me to see if I need anything.

It's Tuesday a.m. and I am back in the surgeon's office for my follow-up and stitches removal. I get to see the surgical area clearly now. The surgeon really did a great job cutting around the areola. In time, I will hardly be able to tell anything was done there. Funny the things I worry about.

The surgeon explains that although the calcifications on my mammography are benign, it led them to more areas of atypical hyperplasia (ALH), which are not usually associated with calcifications. She points to where the hyperplasia is located on the films and explains the calcifications were like stars. She says she basically had to lift up my breast tissue to get to the spot under them that had the hyperplasia. I start to cry. All I can think of is the night months earlier when I heard God say, "I love you and am with you" while I looked up at the black sky filled with stars.

My prognosis is that I am in a high-risk group for breast cancer. I need to be watched closely and tested every six months, which means more mammograms! The breast surgeon discusses Tamoxifen with me, an oral treatment used to help reduce the development of breast cancer in high-risk women. It is usually taken for five years and helps block the effects of estrogen on certain tissue such as the breast. While Tamoxifen is beneficial for many women, I weigh the risks and benefits for me and decline the treatment, not wanting to put myself into an early menopause and possibly increase my risk of endometrial cancer. I make the decision to wait for six months before having anything more done. In my mind, I just want to get off the "hamster wheel" and take a break. I want to believe this nightmare is over – that all the "bad tissue" is gone. My next mammogram isn't for another six months and I secretly hope it will be nothing more than a routine screening. Except for the continuous vigilance and extra testing, my life can finally get back to normal.

Spring is in full bloom and I am feeling like the season – transformed, energized, encouraged and ready to start anew. I decide to do a spiritual fast, which involves abstaining from certain foods while focusing on prayer. I purchase the book, "The Daniel Fast" by Susan Gregory, recommended by a friend who fasted with members of her church during the previous Lenten season. The twenty-one day fast is modeled after the Daniel principle of eating only what comes from "pulse" or seed, that is, foods that are grown and not processed. I shop for all the approved foods and try to decide what my prayer focus will be during the fast. I have a few things in mind – the health of my breasts, lifting my son Daniel up in prayer as he prepares for his upcoming confirmation, and a recent request for me to lead a new ministry. I begin to keep a journal of my fast.

Here are some of the things I learn:

- I am strong with God
- I can break habits
- I can live led by the Spirit
- I can conquer my fleshly desires
- God is my comfort
- I can do more with God than by myself
- God knows what is best for me
- I am content

One morning as I read the devotional section of "The Daniel Fast," I am encouraged by the author's suggestion to identify "five stones" – analogous to the stones David held when he was up against Goliath. In the context of the book, the stones are used as a metaphor for the biblical verses you hold onto in times of strife or struggle to give you strength when faced with a battle.

The verses I identify are those that help me to trust God, give me strength, hope and confidence, as well as ones focused on protection, humility and obedience.

1. *Proverbs 3:5, 6 (my life verse): Trust in the Lord with all your heart, lean not on your own understanding. In all your ways, acknowledge Him and He will lead your paths straight.*

2. *Philippians 4:13 (a verse my son gave me): I can do all things through Christ who strengthens me.*

3. *Jeremiah 29:11: For I know the plans I have for you says the Lord, plans to give you a hope and a future and not to harm you.*

4. *Psalm 91:11 (a verse Dan and I identified as ours after an accident years prior): He will command His angels to guard you in all your ways.*

5. *Psalm 131:1-3: My heart is not proud; I do not concern myself with great matters or things too wonderful for me. But I have stilled and quieted my soul; like a weaned child with its mother. O Israel, put your hope in the Lord both now and forever more.*

I repeat these over and over again on some days when I get lost in worry. The word of God is truth and something on which I can stand firm. So I move on, hopeful and at peace.

The fast ends the day before Daniel's confirmation. We have a wonderful ceremony at the church and a feast with family and friends at our favorite Italian restaurant. I think all my prayers have been answered.

One of my intentions during the fast is whether to accept a request to lead a new ministry. While I realize I have a heart for many ministries, the most compelling is children and the assurance that they are raised with the love and guidance of the Lord. I decide to commit myself to the new ministry. The class will focus on biblical values for the mothers of students who attend the church's preschool. The board members accept my suggestion to call the group Harvesting Hope. I love the name. It's catchy and uses alliteration and it really speaks to our need for hope. We need to gather hope like a long awaited crop ready to be plucked and feasted on. I hope to offer a place for these women to mature and grow in their faith and I feel blessed by the bond I form with them.

I enjoy the next few months with my family and do a little gardening, which results in my getting poison sumac. The visit to the dermatologist to treat my allergic reaction leads to the identification of a few moles on my back that need to be removed. I have the moles cut out and begin to feel like a piece of moldy cheese that is in constant need of trimming.

Other than a few visits to the dermatologist, the summer is normal and fun and includes a vacation with Dan's parents to Branson, Missouri in August. We see a few shows, play mini golf and rent a boat for a day on the lake. I am healed enough now to resume normal activities. I go tubing with the kids and laugh hysterically as I bounce around behind the boat, hanging on for dear life. We join a group of people that have anchored to climb a landmass jutting out of the water. The kids and I dive out of the boat, swim to the rocks, climb up and jump into the lake. I even try zip lining and glide through the air hands free. I am living my life again. Actually, I am living life like never before!

Chapter 7

A Negative Mood,
A Positive Choice

The summer seems to fly by and soon it's time to get the kids ready for the upcoming school year. The first day of school starts with great excitement. I stand in the driveway, camera in hand, snapping away as John and Daniel, handsome in their uniform chinos and dress shirts, get in the car and take off for the high school. John is now a senior and in only one more year he'll be off to college. Daniel is just starting high school as a freshman.

The boys will be playing sports together this year; Daniel is the Homecoming Prince and John and his girlfriend are the Homecoming King and Queen. No one has to convince me I have a house full of princes! Before I know it, John will have his prom, graduation and will get his driver's license when he turns eighteen.

Our wonderful summer is but a memory and I have had five straight months of no talk of breasts. My routine is changing. I am getting very close to a new season in my life. I enjoy the change of climate and the colors and crisper temperatures of autumn. The transformation of the leaves as they change their hues and descend to the ground remind me this is a time for letting go and relinquishing things that have been burdensome. I am hopeful in my anticipation of the upcoming holidays and gratefully long to close a year that began with a lump.

Since my mornings are now free of providing rides to school, I allow myself a new routine of driving to Panera's for a cup of coffee and some time alone with my bible and journal before heading to the gym. God's word and coffee – perfect together! Each day I station myself at a little corner table near the front window where I can view people coming and going.

I make some new friends as well. Nearby sits a group of men and women who meet every morning. Each day we greet one another and sometimes they draw me into their conversations.

One of the women taught my son Daniel when he was in middle school. She notices my bible and asks what I do there each day. I explain that I read and then journal my personal thoughts as well as keep up with prayer requests. She tells me she and her friends attend mass at the local Roman Catholic Church daily, have breakfast and then go to work. Intrigued by my prayer requests, she shares with me a story about a friend who has breast cancer and asks if I can pray for her as well. I share how by keeping the names of people in my book, I am able to remember them in prayer and am blessed to see God's work in their lives. I disclose my recent year and as she takes my arm, she promises to pray for me at mass each day. I am touched by her generosity.

As the fall wears on, my normal cheery mood experiences some challenges. While I am convinced I can handle the additional mammograms and the close scrutiny, a sense of sadness comes over me. I don't know if it is PMS (premenstrual syndrome), PMDD (premenstrual dysphoric disorder), premenopause, perimenopause or maybe just pure depression. There are days when I succumb to dark or depressing thoughts and I need an extra boost to get out of it. Right now, the little things in life, the mundane, seem to be pulling me down. I need to rebuke these thoughts and change the channel in my head. The devil is a liar and when I have thoughts like these, I need to marry them up with my knowledge of God. Exercise seems to help so I go to the gym as often as I can.

One day at the gym, a woman I casually know stops me and asks how I am, mentioning she hasn't seen me lately. Instead of replying with a nonchalant, "Yeah, I've been busy," I proceed in my typical chattiness to share my unusually taxing year. A mélange of biopsies, partial mastectomy (a term I am now more comfortable with), the removal of two suspicious moles from my back and a case of poison sumac has left me little to no time for keeping my regular gym schedule. The mention of a partial mastectomy prompts her to ask a few additional questions about my situation. She tells me I missed a recent talk she gave about the need for breast cancer screening. She belongs to an organization called FORCE (Facing Our Risk of Cancer Empowered), a national, nonprofit organization devoted to improving the lives of people and families affected by hereditary breast and ovarian cancer.

Sharing her story with me, I learn no woman in her family has gotten out of her forties alive because of breast cancer.

Due to the probability that she too would experience this fate, she opted for a prophylactic bilateral mastectomy with reconstruction. A prophylactic bilateral mastectomy, or preventive removal of the breasts, is an option chosen by women who have an increased risk of developing breast cancer. Among the highest risk groups are those women with a significant family history of breast cancer and those with a known genetic predisposition to the disease.

I stare at her in amazement and ponder my own situation. What if I end up with breast cancer? What if the next mammogram reveals additional potentially life-threatening problems? How will I be able to handle it? How will my family handle it? Sometimes I even think maybe I should just die so my family would not have to bear the burden of my journey. (Yes, sadly I thought that!) But now, after learning about this woman's operation and bravery, I realize I must stop feeling sorry for myself. Because of this woman's kind outreach and her acknowledgment that I had been missed, I realize I do matter and how ridiculous I am being. I, like this woman, want to live and will do everything in my power to make the right decisions and do what I need to stay alive. I leave with a new spirit and a new friend.

God has the ability to place people in our lives without us even realizing why. They are not there by chance or coincidence; they are there for a reason. We may need them to assist us on a difficult journey, a journey we can't envision or may not even choose. They may seem like a godsend and they are. They are there for the times we need them to be.

We can have a truly amazing effect on others' lives. When we practice acts of kindness such as a warm smile, a considerate gesture, or perhaps a friendly compliment, we focus our attention onto someone else. Research shows that being kind to others increases our own levels of happiness as well as theirs and simply makes us feel good. It validates us as human beings.

I come to realize that my overwhelming anxiety is really fear of the future – my next mammogram and beyond. That night I write in my journal: We may not always know where we are going, but we can be confident that we are headed to a beautiful place if we trust God.

Colossians 4:6 ESV: Let your speech always be gracious, seasoned with salt, so that you may know how you ought to answer each person.

Chapter 8

He Prepares Us If We Let Him

I t is early December. A few more days and I will go back to the breast center for yet another mammogram. This is just a precaution but the reality of being a "high risk" patient on a "high watch" list is starting to wear me down. I have enjoyed the past few months of no procedures, no tests and no worries. As I sit in Panera's drinking my coffee, with my journal and my bible, I watch as people drift in. My friends, the other morning "regulars," have come to know my story and continue to pray for me. Their prayers, as well as the prayers of so many others bring me comfort, ammunition in a way.

As I sip the wonderful hazelnut brew, my thoughts travel back to the day before Thanksgiving, four years earlier. That

November, Dan had a life-threatening accident at work, falling thirty feet through the shaft of a tower crane. It was a terrifying day for all of us, but a day of miracles as well. Despite multiple injuries, including a fractured hip, he survived and would heal in many ways in the months to come.

Dan's accident was a huge growing experience for us both. Blessed in many ways during that difficult time, we had many people helping us through their prayers, providing food (especially from my Yadas), money and assistance with the kids. We couldn't have done it alone.

During the healing process, we would read Scripture. One morning soon after we had come home from the hospital, I was led to *Psalm 91:11*. I declare it to this day as a prayer of safety for my family – *For He will command His angels concerning you to guard you in all your ways.*

Months later, right before Dan returned to work (an amazing miracle in itself), I was in New York City with my son Daniel. Finding myself two blocks away from the site of the accident, I felt an incredible urge to walk to the spot where Dan fell. After all these months, the building remained unfinished and the tower crane could still be seen rising hundreds of feet into the air and reaching out just as far. As I peered straight up to the top of the structure, I shuttered at the thought of what happened on that day months earlier. I also realized that the enormity of the crane is in no way a comparison to the enormity of God. Thankful for Dan's recovery, I raised my hand in praise, bowed my head and prayed, "My God is so much bigger than you," reciting the verse in *Proverbs 18:10: The name of the Lord is a strong tower; the righteous man runs into it and is safe.*

I am brought back from my reverie to my usual table in Panera's. The steam from my coffee swirls around my growing smile as I remind myself God is bigger than any mountain, structure or disease I may face. God is bigger than cancer. Just like that time after Dan's accident, I find myself thankful for God's faithfulness. I remember that even in difficult situations, such as this past year, I can find peace and joy as I draw closer to God. He will be with me on this next visit to the breast center, as always.

Monday arrives and it is time for my mammogram. The ride to the breast center is stressful. Traffic this morning is horrendous. What should take forty-five minutes is drawing close to two hours. I call the breast center to let them know I am stuck in traffic, secretly hoping they will tell me to turn around and go home. Instead, they simply advise me to, "Get here when you can."

When I arrive, a very nice young woman takes my personal information and insurance cards and as she does, I compliment her on a pin she is wearing. The pin holds a photo of a little boy, which she proudly tells me is her son. Both mothers of sons, I share with her some motherly advice and promise to keep her son in my prayers.

Escorted back to the dressing room, I begin the all too familiar routine. I put on the soft, warm, fluffy robe again, knowing it's a ruse. I may look like I am about to have a spa treatment – but I am not! A cup of comforting coffee or tea, a magazine and a warm robe do nothing to mask what I know is coming.

I go into the waiting room and stare at the TV screen until I am led to the exam room for my first round of "pictures." After the mammogram I am instructed to remain in the room. The technician returns a few minutes later and nonchalantly says, "The radiologist wants a few more pictures." Just some more pictures? This is not my idea of a photo shoot. The left, then the right. A few more. I feel my stress level escalating. I want to scream and hit the innocent technician who is just doing her job. Instead I firmly say, "I am done! I want to see the radiologist. I am not getting squashed in this machine one more time!" As the technician lets me out of the torture chamber, I pull my robe tightly against me and frantically start texting Dan, *Something is wrong, they want to do more tests!* He texts me back, *Relax.* Despite my shaky hands, I start scribbling all kinds of questions on a piece of paper as I wait for the radiologist to join me. My mind, my intellect needs to take charge. I need to acquire information. Something is not right. I am overtaken with fear and the bad memories of the early part of this year.

The technician comes back and leads me to a consult room. A radiologist I have never met and the patient navigator from months earlier greet me. The radiologist kindly answers my questions and politely explains that based on my history and what she can see on the films taken today, they will need to do more stereotactic biopsies to verify the increased calcifications that are present. How can there be more calcifications? I thought I took care of this? I ask questions to feel some sense of command over the situation as my life spirals out of control. I write down the answers to my questions and additional information from the patient navigator on genetic counselors. Before I leave, I arrange a consult with my breast surgeon so that the biopsies can be scheduled. I drive home. No traffic. Just a lot on my mind. I send out another email to my "team" when I arrive home.

December 12, 2011

Subject: It's Always Something ...

Hey all!

Eight months have gone by since my last surgery. Last spring was filled with multiple biopsies, bilateral partial mastectomy, etc. I just had my six-month mammography and here we are again with more calcifications of the same nature. Unfortunately the way they monitor me is not the most "fun" or should I just say, "patient friendly" and I do not want to be in a cycle of being a piece of moldy cheese needing to be trimmed and put back in the fridge! But I am thankful and praise God that whatever I have is in its early stages.

I saw the surgeon today after the mammogram and I need another MRI and possibly more biopsies. The type of condition I have is not yet cancer, but seems to develop into it. We discussed all options including a mastectomy. I even have a little pamphlet on what to expect. We will continue after Christmas, starting with the MRI. I can go into the stats and options, but would rather not. I just want to pray and discuss this with Dan and the doctors and see where God leads us.

Initially I was very shocked, let down and even afraid. God knows how I feel, but I also know what a great and awesome God He is and He is faithful to bring me through whatever I will need to do.

I ask that you pray for wisdom and strength for me as I continue my journey, and the healing I will need no matter what I have to do. If you are getting this message, it is because I love you and value your friendship.

A friend of mine posted this verse today on Facebook. I love it! It is from 2 Timothy 1:12: I know in whom I believe, Jesus Christ, and am confident that He is able to guard what I have entrusted to Him for that day.

Two friends, Patti and Elaine, are pushing me to get a second opinion. After receiving my email, Elaine calls to offer some advice and encouragement. She shares that she is praying for me and feels strongly that I consult other physicians. At first, I hesitate in my normal task-oriented way of approaching things. I have had a phenomenal experience with my chosen breast surgeon. Using her amazing skills, she helped me through a successful surgery last April and the thought of starting over with another surgeon seems unnecessary and onerous to me.

But Elaine presses on. She says she walked another dear friend through this same process and helped her search for doctors. She recommends I meet the surgeon her friend chose to perform her surgery. I concede and tell her I will think about it.

Later, as I contemplate choosing a new surgeon, I get consumed with concerns such as costs, insurance, the logistics and the downtime. I look up the two doctors Elaine recommends on the Internet. Their profiles are impressive. I also have to consider my current surgeon is not in my insurance plan's network and I have no idea what the costs will be if I use her again, especially considering the surgeries are getting more involved and expensive. While we were able to work out a payment plan for the last surgery, I have a child getting ready to go to college. My recovery will necessitate that I take time off from work too. The more I think about it, I realize that it is time to consider our personal finances and getting a second opinion is a very sound and rationale thing to do. I plan to follow through with the MRI, but start searching the web, reading testimonials and looking at before and after pictures of surgeries. Trusting Elaine's judgment and opinion, I decide to make an appointment with another breast surgeon. In my mind, I think this is just my due diligence. But, I also know the advice and prayers of my friends have enlightened me at times before my own wisdom.

I send this to the group after my "Christmas MRI":

> *MRI came back with no invasiveness. It also went much better this time. I had less nausea and the intravenous was put into my arm as opposed to my hand. I need to talk to the surgeon about future biopsies/surgeries. I am tired.*

> *Have a wonderful New Year – cheers in 2012!*

> *May you all look back on 2011 praising God for His faithfulness and goodness and look forward to 2012 trusting in Him and putting your hope in Him.*

> *Love,*
> *Barb*

As I await the follow-up discussion with the breast surgeon, I call and schedule a consult with another surgeon. She is in my insurance plan's network and very well known with more than forty years experience. She specializes in breast health, breast surgery and surgical oncology. Her office manager and nurse are lovely on the phone and sound very competent. They explain that I need to request all my lab pathologies, mammography films and MRIs from the other institutions and bring them with me to my consult appointment. This doctor is part of a different hospital and breast center so I make all the necessary phone calls, write the letters I need for the lab release and pick up my films from the original breast center. Everything is set in motion so the new surgeon will have all the required information before my first appointment on January 27th.

The day of my appointment there is a torrential downpour. I plan on going to the appointment alone, but miraculously, Dan's car pulls in the driveway just as I'm about to leave. Due to the weather, the construction job has shut down early. Dan walks in, gives me a kiss and says he can go with me. Divine intervention again? Grateful for the company and the moral support, I drive with Dan to the breast surgeon's office.

Originally I am nonchalant about the appointment, thinking I am just going through the motions, checking the "get a second opinion" box. As I sit in the waiting room, I feel strangely at peace. I meet eyes with a few patients; their bright smiles belie whatever they are battling.

After a brief wait, a nurse greets Dan and me, and leads us to an exam room. I answer a few questions for her as she jots down some notes and then leaves me to get undressed. I put on the obligatory "open in front" cotton gown and hop up onto the exam table. I swing my feet like a little kid, and wait, hoping maybe this visit I will leave with just a lollipop and no more. Dan smiles but we speak little of why we are here.

After a gentle knock, the door opens as a small, sweet grand-motherly looking woman enters. She confidently approaches and shakes our hands. She takes a few moments to look over the chart, films and past reports I brought with me. We review what has transpired over the past year. She asks about my anxiety, what the past year has been like and what was going on with my family. We talk at length about my family history and the strong prevalence of hormonal cancers. She turns to Dan and asks him some questions about his feelings, his experience and even his own health. I like the fact that she includes him. As Dan talks, I feel the surgeon taking it all in and slowly absorbing our experience with interest and concern. Like it or not, Dan is fast becoming a breast cancer husband – the kind of husband that wants desperately to be emotionally supportive yet feels helpless at times in light of the imminent possibility of breast surgery or worse. We discuss various routes that may be taken. One includes a mastectomy, but she says she has not made a final decision on that yet. I share that although I am not looking forward to it, I am concerned I may be on an inevitable cycle of biopsies and lumpectomies, aka partial mastectomies. She encourages me to at least make an appointment to meet one of the plastic surgeons she works with closely. She hands me his card and says he does beautiful work, even referring to him as an artist. There is something about her confident yet humble manner that draws me to her and makes me feel calm. I thank her and she hugs me, promising to review all of my results and call me soon.

Before leaving, her nurse returns to tell us the doctor has ordered genetic testing as well, which will determine if I have inherited the harmful mutation of the BRCA1 gene or the

BRCA2 gene, increasing my risk of developing breast and/or ovarian cancer. The nurse explains that it is a DNA test that involves swabbing my inner cheek. The doctor wants to obtain results from this test as she considers my next course of action.

Dan helps me put on my coat and we leave. On the way to the car I look at him and say "I really like her" and he agrees. We are especially touched by the fact that she talks to both of us as individuals but tells us that since God has joined us to be one flesh, she treats us as one. That means so much to us and at that moment we decide she is "our" new breast surgeon. When we get home, I write my first surgeon a note and earnestly thank her for her care over the past year. She was a godsend.

During our discussions, my new surgeon picks up on the fact that this past year has exacerbated my stress and anxiety levels. She prescribes Xanax, a drug to help alleviate symptoms of anxiety and panic and tells me to take it if I feel I need it. I fill the prescription, but in the end, never take any. Over the years I have been predisposed to anxiety, but have always been functional. God's word has been instrumental in helping me and I have tried very hard to pray more fervently when I get anxious. This verse says it all in *Philippians 4:6: Do not be*

anxious about anything, but in every situation, by prayer and peti-
tion, with thanksgiving, present your requests to God.

A week goes by and still no call from the breast surgeon. I am anxiously awaiting the DNA results and her conclusions, but I want to be proactive so I make an appointment with the plastic surgeon. I plan on going alone, but today there is a torrential downpour again! Dan's car pulls in the driveway moments before I have to leave. As he enters the house, Dan says he will drive me to my appointment. I tell him I feel like I am going to see the Wizard of Oz – "Oh mighty Oz, can I please have two new healthy breasts?" We laugh and I cry a little too.

We finally arrive at the plastic surgeon's office despite the horrible weather. It is pristine and stylishly decorated. Several diplomas and awards hang on the office walls, but I am particularly taken with the aesthetic graphite drawings in large frames. It turns out they are sketches done by the surgeon over the years. He truly is an artist!

After finishing my new patient paperwork, Dan and I are led to a comfortable office where a tall, thin, handsome man with a ready smile stands and greets us. He is impeccably dressed and exudes confidence, and I immediately dub him "Dr. Dapper." Extending his hand, he welcomes us with a friendly, competent handshake. We all settle into big leather chairs and I share my story with him, explaining that a mastectomy and reconstruction could be part of my future so this consult is important to me. Since I have small breasts, the potential for more lumpectomies could be disfiguring or pose additional complications for future reconstruction if I ultimately need it. While I wasn't planning on a mastectomy or reconstruction, I was preparing myself in case this is the road I would have to travel. After hearing about my last few procedures, Dr. Dapper starts to explain what his role would be. He is very self assured, but not arrogant. He speaks to both Dan and I and his demeanor and empirical knowledge are comforting to me. We see "before" and "after" pictures of various breast reconstruction patients on his computer screen. He even has sample expanders and implants on his desk and explains the difference between silicone and saline, if I were to opt for implants. I pick up a silicone one and start to nervously play with it. I give it to Dan and he turns red. The doctor assures me he has had many patients in my shoes with similar histories. Although he has a few routes he could take, he cautions us that he would still like to wait and see what the breast surgeon advises. He does however want to continue the consult with a physical exam so we are led into another room where I need to undress and put on a gown in the usual fashion – "open in front."

After a few minutes, Dr. Dapper enters and asks me to stand in front of him. I am embarrassed and cringe at how intimidating it is to stand naked in front of a total stranger while he and his nurse proceed to take meticulous measurements of most of my torso. I learn I do not have many options for reconstruction because of my slight frame. Basically I do not have enough "extra" tissue to do an autologous breast reconstruction. Autologous reconstruction would use parts of muscle and fat tissue from either my back or stomach to create a new breast. My choice for reconstruction includes silicone or saline implants placed in a pocket made below my chest muscles. One especially important fact we learn is that since I am at high risk for breast cancer, the nipple would have to go as well if I get a mastectomy. This is because the tissue is vulnerable to cancer. I have heard there are some procedures called "nipple sparing," but based on the fact that the tissue would need to be monitored because of risk, this doesn't seem like an option.

Dr. Dapper finishes his exam and Dan and I complete a few more forms and then consult with the office manager. She reviews the office process with us if we should decide we need the services of the plastic surgeon. We leave feeling very comfortable.

When I arrive home I start scanning the Internet. I look at pictures on the surgeon's web page in the privacy of my own den. He has a whole section of before and after pictures of the different types of reconstruction he performs. It's hard to look at, but I do. I start making a habit of it every night. It is somewhat morbid, but eventually the shock wears off and I start to acclimate myself with the after pictures. The end results are actually amazing and light years ahead of the options available to women in years past. After the scars fade, it will be hard to tell these women even had a mastectomy.

One evening, I start to Google other sites and get hooked on blogs that some women have posted. Most of what I see and read is related to progress after surgery, the experience, complications, etc. All complete with selfies! They are not pretty as they seem to highlight the worst parts of their recuperation. Feeling dejected, I start to cry. My son Daniel walks in and seeing me asks, "What's the matter mom?" I say "Nothing. I'm okay." He knows something is wrong, but says okay and kisses me goodnight. The academic in me starts to look at every picture on the web and read every blog imaginable. Each night I do this until I am exhausted and when I go to bed I neglect to pray. I am truly not myself.

One afternoon, I remember the plastic surgeon's offer to put me in touch with some former patients whose situations were similar to my own. I call the office and explain how I would really appreciate speaking to someone. While this may not help everyone, I find personal testimonies to be valuable when making important decisions. The woman they put me in touch with is a godsend. She answers all my questions and our conversation helps me as she reaffirms many of my feelings.

In addition to research, consults, opinions and personal testimonies, the pages thereafter in my journal all express my most important resource – prayer and God's word. I ask for guidance, for strength to make decisions and for discernment and wisdom as I look at all the possible options. In the end,

I know my prayers are so important because despite all the data, results and doctors' advice, I will only have true peace if I include God in my decision. I write in my journal: When we ask God, we get wisdom. When we ask others, we may just get an opinion. I also stop going to bed without praying.

> *Know also that wisdom is sweet to your soul; if*
> *you find it, there is a future hope for you, and your*
> *hope will not be cut off. Proverbs 24:14 ESV*

Chapter 9

God Sometimes Asks Us To Do Crazy Things

I continue to pray as I wait for my new breast surgeon to assess all the relevant information and call me with her recommendation on how we should proceed. Her call comes one night in mid-February. I see her name pop up on the television screen and immediately run to grab the phone. As I hold the phone to my left ear, Dan sits scrutinizing me, trying to figure out what the doctor is saying. I hang up the phone and just stand there, pursing my lips together. Without warning my shoulders begin to shake and I start to cry. Dan comes to me, gathers me in his arms and kisses my head. I thought I prepared myself for this moment. I wrote about it and discussed it over and over with loved ones until I convinced myself it was inevitable. I even joked about it. However, it wasn't until this phone call that it really sinks in and becomes real. Before I go to bed, I email my friends. I have to tell them I am going to have a bilateral mastectomy.

February 12, 2012

Subject: The Mother of All Biopsies!

Hey all! I just got off the phone with the breast surgeon. I will be scheduling a mastectomy. I am breathing a sigh of relief now that I have an answer and am standing in awe of how God has worked all things together.

In this short time, I have found the surgeons I will use, had another mammography and also got the results on the BRCA testing which were negative. That is great news! It lessens worries for ovarian cancer; however, I still can't ignore what is brewing in my breasts. Dan was able to come

*on all the visits with me to make these decisions.
I also have had such prayer support and good
friends that have encouraged me and helped me
in this process.*

*With each test, they keep finding more ALH. This
gives me a one in three risk of breast cancer and
with my young age—wink, wink—and the need for
continued invasive monitoring and more biopsies,
I have opted for this. The surgeon confirms that I
would ultimately be picked apart with each sub-
sequent lumpectomy and the plastic surgeon said
that eventually reconstruction would become more
difficult because of scar tissue from each procedure.*

*I truly believe God gave me a gift of finding this
early. Remember this all started with a lump – a
benign lump that was aspirated and eventually
disappeared. But the testing to follow up on that
lump resulted in all that I went through over the*

past twelve months which possibly contributed to saving my life.

Please continue to pray for a successful surgery, no cancer in the lymph nodes (they will biopsy the sentinel nodes the day of surgery) and healing. The complete reconstruction process will take multiple surgeries over the coming year, but God willing, I will not need any chemotherapy or radiation. That will be determined on the day of surgery after all pathologies come back. Date is TBD. More to come.

Love,

Barb

That night I write in my journal:

I am confused! I have spent this year growing in trust of You – You who are all trustworthy. I truly believe You have led me to this place, yet now I am scared and hesitant. How can this be? Please Lord, give me the strength and courage and confidence in You to continue this journey, one I believe You put me on. I love You.

The next day I send this email to a few select friends:

February 13, 2012

Subject: Am I Crazy?

OK – after all is said and done, I am now getting scared. Am I really doing this? I felt like I made all the right decisions, and now that it is almost "go" time, I want to say "stop!" Am I crazy? Why is this happening?

These are some of their responses:

From my best friend:

Oh Barb. I am sending you hugs. I think you need to take a deep breath, and, as I like to say, "hang it on the cross." Don't read blogs, take time to process the decision. It will all be okay!

XOXO,

P.

From a friend whose mother died young from breast cancer:

You are absolutely not crazy! YOU are brave and smart to make this decision and face this head on. Of course you are scared – you are making a decision to save your life – and you are doing everything right, my friend. I love you!

M.

From a friend who lost her best friend to breast cancer:

No you're not crazy ... you're normal! I read your email today and I waited to respond, mainly because I wasn't sure what to say. Don't get me wrong, I was totally impressed with how strong and confident you sounded. I was in awe that you were so matter of fact, that you had made your decisions, you knew they were the right ones and you were going full steam ahead. Secretly I was wishing I had your faith. Then things would be easy.

But these things are never easy. First of all, it's devastating to have to make these types of decisions. Even with Dan's support, your family and friends, and God's, it's still difficult. You're human and that means you may have doubts, you may need some more time to think about things, or even if you're sure of your decision, you may just need some time to get used to everything that's about to happen. It's human to be scared.

This is what is real — you are the most wonderful, loving, caring, intelligent and spiritual person I know. Trust in yourself that whatever decision you make, it will be the right one. God will help you. But never, ever feel that making any decision, even the right one, means you can't have doubts or be nervous. It's at those times that those who love you will pray harder. I know I am.

If you ever want to talk, day or night, pick up the phone and call me. I promise to listen to your voice and your heart.

H.

What wonderful, encouraging friends I have! I so treasure them.

After one last call to my surgeon, I send this email:

February 14, 2012

Subject: Needing reassurance

I just got off the phone with the surgeon. As you know, I had a freak out moment where the decision I made went from my "logical/scientific" mind to my heart and I thought, "What am I doing?" She told me I am totally normal and if I didn't feel this way she would think I was nuts. She said the February date is still TBD because she is still awaiting the actual pathology slides from the first hospital to confirm the pervasiveness of the ALH, etc. She will call me when she has seen everything. The best part was that at the end of the call she asked if I had a moment to pray with her. It was the most beautiful prayer asking for healing and acknowledging our creator as healer. This woman is amazing – she told me all she wants to be is

God's instrument in this process if needed. I am at peace again and awaiting the next step as God goes before me to lead.

The next day, I meet the woman I have befriended from the gym. I tell her of my decision to remove both breasts and mention the names of my chosen surgeons. She smiles because unbelievably, she has experience with these surgeons as well and confirms they are excellent in their fields. Coincidence or divine intervention? I think I see another fingerprint of God in my life.

Chapter 10

Stay Humble, Seek Wisdom

February 18, 2012

Subject: Date soon!

*Hey all. I just got off the phone with the surgeon
again. After reviewing all of my results from last
year, she feels very strongly that I should do this.
There are enough spots that are "active" with
growth in my left breast and other changes in
my right (all this activity in such a small area!).
Anyway, her office will probably call within the
next few days to schedule my operation. I truly*

see how God has led me and prepared me for this;
even these last two weeks have been significant to
me. God is with me. His wisdom is what I will
follow. I continue to ask for strength and healing
and praise God for His faithfulness to me!

Love you,
Barb

The next day the surgeon's office manager calls to give me an appointment for the operation and reconstruction. I take out my planner, page to March 7th and mark the date. While I am not sure of the exact date when puberty started for me, I can now tell you the exact day I got breasts! In my heart I feel confidence and peace that I made the right decision. I start to count down the days until the operation and start to give the house a good spring cleaning. I'm just an ordinary woman on any regular day cleaning the house. However, it's been a long time since anything was regular in my life. I plan to clean everything including the much neglected shelves in my curio and china cabinet. I wash curtains and move furniture.

Even the dog gets washed. I'm not sure of the exact protocol but I think one must need an immaculate house before a major operation. I also go to the gym faithfully so that I can be as fit as possible prior to surgery as I know a stronger body will make for an easier recovery.

The week prior to surgery, I need pre-op screening and a physical to be cleared for a long day in the operating room. The internist performs an EKG and draws the required blood for testing. They confirm that the results will be forwarded to the hospital. I later discover from the surgeon that the EKG reveals I have mitral valve prolapse. Now I need to see a cardiologist to get clearance before next Wednesday. Another bump in the road! I take down the information and declare I am foregoing healthy living, and am going to start smoking, do drugs and possibly join a commune!

The most encouraging words come from the plastic surgeon on my final visit before the surgery. His nurse has to take the obligatory "before" photos and we have one last discussion about what the reconstruction will entail: visits for expansion to stretch the tissue, the exchange surgery to get the implants, and nipple reconstruction. I listen intently and feel the enormity of his task. With tears in my eyes, I look at him and ask, "You are going to put me back together, right? My son is graduating this year and I have to be there. And, Dan and I promised the boys we would take them to Aruba this summer …" My voice starts to trail off. He is jotting down some notes in my file but stops to look up at me. He puts his pen down, takes my hand and with warm eyes and an equally warm smile says, "You are going to be fine. You are not only going to enjoy all those things, I promise you are going to look fabulous on the beach as well."

On Sunday, I meet Kristina, a friend from church who is a labor and delivery nurse at the medical center where I will be having surgery. She tells me she is praying for me and assures me the anesthesiologists are great.

Monday (T minus 2 days!): I meet the cardiologist and he is awesome! A soft-spoken man, he assures me everything will be okay and that he too has had patients who have undergone mastectomies and are doing well. Due to my mitral valve prolapse with regurgitation, I have now become a regular under his watchful eye to make sure my heart stays healthy!

March 6, 2012: While by myself, on my last "normal" morning for a while, I sip my coffee at Panera's and read today's journal entry aloud. It's really more of a prayer to God than a recital of words on a page. I ask God for the surgery to go well, that there will be no clotting issues in my legs or other complications, that the lymph nodes will be clear and that I heal well afterwards. I also pray for provision for the bills. I praise God for the pre-test results and how far He has taken me thus far.

I begin to think back to when I was a little girl in the fifth grade. I was on the swim team and my dad would drive me to and from practice every Wednesday night. Some of the girls on the team started picking on me. My dad had always told me never to pick a fight with anyone, but that I should always stick up for myself. When he heard about their teasing, he began to stay and watch me for the whole practice. His presence always made me feel safe. In the same way, I feel like breast cancer is picking a fight with me and my Heavenly Father is watching and He will make me feel safe. I thank Him for the army of prayer warriors that I know is lifting me up in prayer and for the angels I know He commands to be by my side. Knowing the next day will be a long day in surgery, I add this verse to my journal:

Exodus 14:14: The Lord will fight for you, you need only be still.

Less than twenty-four hours to go. A few close friends call to check on me and we pray together for peace and for all to go well. My sisters and my fifteen-month-old niece spend the day with me. We go to lunch where my niece entertains me and reminds me how irrepressibly charming toddlers can be. After lunch, we drive to the same playground I frequented with my boys when they were small. I run around with my niece and it feels good to forget about the impending operation and enjoy the spontaneity of having a nice, normal day. We head to the local mall where my sisters, the ultimate shoppers, help me acquire my new wardrobe for the coming months. Yoga pants, stretchy camisoles that I can step into and inch up my body so as not to reach overhead, a few tops that open in front and a pair of "sensible" slip on shoes. Not my preferred fashion pieces.

We arrive home and my sisters and niece have dinner with me, Dan and the boys. We hug and kiss as they leave and they assure me they will visit me at the hospital after the operation. They ask if I am afraid. By this time, I am not. I think about what

God says three hundred and sixty-five times in the bible: *do not be afraid/fear not*. I look over the verses Linda sent to me the day after I initially found the lump. They still mean so much to me.

At approximately 7 p.m. the anesthesiologist calls to explain the type of medications he will administer and reassures me he will be by my side the whole time to monitor my very low blood pressure. I tell him I am all set with the medication for tonight and tomorrow morning to combat any potential nausea post surgery, and I have filled the prescriptions for pain and possible infection. I pack a small bag with my new clothes, a lunch for Dan and before I go to bed, I log on to Facebook and change my profile picture to a pair of pink boxing gloves and write a status update:

> *I am cleared for surgery tomorrow. I realize I am not brave or strong, but through the Word of God, prayer and God's people, He equips me. These verses are especially with me for the coming days:*

> *Psalm 138:3: On the day I called, You answered me; my strength of soul You increased.*

Exodus 14:14 (2 versions): The LORD will fight for you while you keep silent. / The Lord shall fight for you, and ye shall hold your peace.

Philippians 4:13: I can do all things through Christ who strengthens me.

Little did I know at the time, but a group of alumni from my high school also started praying for me after they saw this post.

Chapter 11

God Knows the Big Picture

March 7, 2012 – 4:30 a.m.: I brush my teeth and fix my hair. I look in the mirror one last time at what will be my former body. I am sad and disappointed thinking how silly I have been criticizing myself all these years. There have been times over this past year where I have flippantly joked about "getting new ones." But, here I stand realizing the phrase "you don't know what you have until it's gone" is very true. I vow to be kinder to myself in the future. I say "goodbye" to my old body and thank it for the memories.

I go into Daniel's room and kiss him. Sleepily, he mumbles he will pray for me today. I then enter John's room and kiss him. He wakes, smiles and asks, "you gonna be okay momma?"

I choke back tears, kiss his forehead and say "I'm gonna be just fine. God didn't bring me this far for nothing!" I walk to the kitchen where Dan is standing ready to get me to the hospital on time.

We leave with my living will signed and sitting on the dining room table, next to a small keepsake book I bought months earlier, titled "My Mom." In my quiet mornings at Panera's I faithfully filled in the answers to the prompting questions in the book, finishing it just before today. If I should die in surgery, I want to leave my sons with some information about myself – things we never had the chance to talk about, pivotal moments in my life, special memories and words of wisdom. It is all part of a huge "letting go" moment of trust with God. I do not want to die. I am going through with this surgery because I want to live. But, I need to come to terms with the fact that if I should die, my family will be okay, because they are still in God's hands. Even though I am a wife and mother, I don't sustain anyone. God sustains us all. I pray if something happens to me, it would draw them closer to Him.

Dan and I arrive at the medical center and park the car. Entering through the big revolving doors, a gentleman greets us and assuming we are headed for the surgical floor, directs us to the elevators. Up a few floors, the doors open and it is eerily peaceful as many of the hospital workers have yet to arrive. We find the registration desk, fill out some papers and wait. A nurse comes and takes us into a room where I will be prepped for surgery. She gives me a pair of paper slippers, a hospital gown and a hair net. She also hands me a plastic cup for a urine sample and points to the bathroom. Vain until the end, I cringe while placing the hair net on my head, put on the cotton gown, place all my clothes in a bag and check myself out in the bathroom mirror. What a sight. The nurse helps me place an anti-nausea patch behind my left ear. I return the plastic cup to her, now filled with a urine sample for a pregnancy test. Though I assure her I am not pregnant she insists on performing the test anyway. She leaves us and we wait for the plastic surgeon. Dan smiles at me and gives me a look that I know says, "I'm sorry you have to go through this." I hug him and we silently watch the morning's news on the overhead television.

Twenty minutes later, Dr. Dapper knocks and enters the room. He is in what appears to be freshly ironed scrubs, but I can tell he has already been busy this morning. He greets Dan and me warmly and explains that he needs to mark me before surgery. I am not exactly sure what the markings tell him, but he confidently uses a black marker and intently maps out his plan for where he will be working. He explains to Dan how the day will proceed and takes Dan's cell number, assuring him he will check in immediately after the operation.

The nurse returns with some blankets and instructs me to lie down on the gurney. As she covers me, she tells me I am going to radiology next. Dan remains in the waiting room as I start to travel through the halls to the radiology department, calmly examining the ceiling tiles. Lit up in the distance I see the radiology sign and am soon deposited in an open area filled with machines. A technician greets me and explains he will be injecting me with a radioactive dye so the surgeon can see where my sentinel nodes and surrounding lymph nodes are located. The machine will monitor when the dye arrives in the lymph nodes near my armpits and breasts. The lymph nodes will be removed during surgery and tested for signs of cancer. The injections are painful. I breathe deeply and tell myself it will be over soon. Once the dye gets settled I will be ready. As I wait for the technician to see what he needs to see on the scanner, a tear falls from my eye. Just then a nurse in radiology comes over and takes my hand. She talks with me and helps me pass the time. Her smile and compassion help to relax me.

I have been pricked and prodded, injected with dyes and needles and surgery hasn't even started. I return to Dan and wait for them to take me to the surgical floor. We watch a little more news and I remind Dan that my dear friend, JP, will arrive at the hospital soon to keep him company. I make sure he has the phone numbers he needs to call with today's updates. I have a phone chain in place for church, the Yadas and family. JP has an email distribution list of my faithful friends and will be writing the emails on my behalf for a while, providing my status updates. JP will be the commander of all communications and report on my status throughout the whole healing process. One of the things I love about JP is that she is able to communicate with my friends easily and comfortably. Even though she has never met them, they soon fall in love with her too. I so enjoy connecting all the great people I love.

Before they take me to surgery, I kiss my husband and pray it will only be a few hours before I see him again. I am ready. God is with me. As I am transported to the operating room, I do not look around. I close my eyes, like a child on a scary ride at the amusement park, anxious and excited, too scared to look.

The gurney stops and I open my eyes. The surgical room must be close by. I turn my head to the left and see the anesthesiologist by my side. He bends over me and says hello. I recognize his voice from our conversation the night before. He takes my hand and assures me he will keep a close watch over me during the entire surgery. As he starts the intravenous into my left hand, I look away. As I do, I see the breast surgeon walking towards me, dressed in her scrubs and ready for surgery. She takes my right hand. I look up at her and thank her for all she has done for me and will do for me today. She smiles sweetly, her warm brown eyes fixed intently on me. I know this woman is a powerhouse of knowledge and experience, but what I see is something more. Somehow I know this woman will perform my surgery gently and with care, just as someone tenderly knits a blanket for a loved one. As I fall into a medicinal sleep, I silently thank God for my operating team, for gifting them with the skills and knowledge to do what they need to do.

JP joins Dan and for hours they watch as people come and go from the hospital waiting room and listen as other patient's family members receive updates from their surgeons. The update board on an overhead screen gives the status about each surgical room to help the family and friends know whether their loved one is still in surgery or in recovery. My board does not change for a long time. After the mastectomy is complete, the breast surgeon comes out and assures Dan and JP all went very well and her part is now over. The plastic surgeon is now starting the process of the first step of reconstruction. By the time the plastic surgeon comes out to talk to Dan, the waiting room is empty, the janitor Dan's only companion.

It is now 10 p.m., seventeen hours since we entered the hospital. Right before I open my eyes in the recovery room, I feel an awakening. I know I am here. I am back. I feel like I have crossed over a chasm. I think of the verse in *Isaiah 43:2*: *When you pass through the waters, I will be with you; and through the rivers, they shall not overwhelm you; when you walk through fire you shall not be burned, and the flame shall not consume you.*

The first person I see is Dan. His reassuring smile gives me the confidence to know I am going to be fine. He kisses me, but looks exhausted. He stays with me until I get into my hospital room. The nurse tells me they have run out of morphine pumps. Full of drugs from the surgery and wrapped tightly, I register pain, but am so happy to be alive. I tell the nurse I will be fine with an injection of a pain medication to quell the discomfort and help me sleep. For now, I require nothing else. Lulled by the squeeze and release of compression cuffs on my legs, the medication kicks in and before I know it, I'm asleep.

The next morning, afraid to move my arms I do the best I can to feel around with my left hand, locating the remote for the hospital bed. A tray with breakfast is suspended like a bridge over my bed. After thirty-six hours of not eating, hospital scrambled eggs and a blueberry muffin look like manna from heaven to me. Unfortunately, I can't reach the tray to get to the food. I start to strain my neck and inch down to the food, but to no avail. Fortunately, to my surprise, my friend Kristina walks in. Laughing at my predicament, she helps me with breakfast. She says she is on her way to work on the labor and delivery floor and wanted to stop in and see how I was doing. She also tells me all the women at bible study prayed for me yesterday. What a blessing! I am so thankful for her thoughtfulness and the time she took out of her day to see me. I am also happy to finally be eating my breakfast!

Just as I finish my muffin, Dan walks in and asks me how I am feeling. He tells me the boys send their love and then proceeds to give me a full report of their night – Chinese food with Grandma and Grandpa and staying up late until Dan could come home with a full report. After being assured the operation was successful and I was fine, they finally went to bed. I plan on calling them after they come home from school today. I can't wait to hear their voices. Both boys played varsity ice hockey this year and there is a hockey banquet tonight. To contribute to the festivities, I made centerpieces for the banquet tables and sent them ahead with a fellow mom and friend. It is my way of feeling I am part of their celebration even though I cannot be with them. Though I am upset about not being there, I am comforted with the thought that I will be attending many more of their life events in the future.

In addition to calling the boys, the other important call I make is to my dad who lives in Florida. I can tell he is relieved to hear my voice. I keep it cheery and upbeat, joking that I will be at the gym and Costco tomorrow. He is happy to hear the operation went well and gives me some fatherly advice: "Rest and heal!" He promises to visit soon. My two sisters arrive as soon as visiting hours start. They tell me they needed to see my face and think I look great. I think it is because I am at peace.

Dan sits with me during the day. We are both tired after the long day yesterday. It's good to be with each other and chat, mindlessly watch a little television and relax as best as possible in a hospital room. Dr. Dapper and his nurse come to check on me. They feel around my chest area to check for swelling and redness. They show me the bandages and assure me all went very well yesterday. While showing Dan how to monitor the drains and manage my medications, the doctor reminds us Monday is my follow-up visit and if there are any questions or problems, he is available on his cell phone. He also leaves instructions for the floor nurse to remove my intravenous and pneumatic compression devices from my calves. I rejoice that my arms are free from their tether and I get ready to leave the bed to take a brief walk. It's hard to get off the bed, but I use my stomach muscles to pull myself up. I become hyper-aware of the plastic drains on each side, sticking out of my upper rib area. They are basically clear plastic tubes, sutured into the area that once was my breast. Near my waist is the end of each tube, small "grenade-like" plastic bulbs that collect fluid and help to decrease swelling and bruising. With Dan by my side, I take a few laps up and down the hallway. I go slowly, arms tight and close to my side, but get tired quickly and return to my bed. Nevertheless, I am proud that I'm able to walk, thinking this is a huge accomplishment. I hear the theme song to "Rocky" in my head and I'm determined to return to my old self as soon as possible.

On Friday, the doctor will discharge me if the drainage is at an acceptable level. I am antsy to get out of the hospital. By mid afternoon we get the news I am to be released. Dan helps me dress into what will be my new uniform for the next few weeks – yoga pants, a camisole and a cardigan that opens in the front. An aide wheels me to the revolving doors that received us just two days earlier. I'm going home! Taking my bag, Dan leaves to get the car. For the next few minutes, I watch the steady flow of people entering the hospital. I wonder where they are going and why are they here. I offer up a short prayer that God will watch over them and all will go well with whatever they are facing. I return my focus to the entranceway as our car pulls up in front. The aide wheels me out to the car and Dan settles me in to the front seat. Much to his dismay, I do not put on my seatbelt. The thought of anything across my chest and possibly tightening around me is too upsetting. He makes me compromise and adjusts it so that it is across my lap and tucks the shoulder strap behind me. My husband, a real New York driver, is navigating through the streets very gingerly. I see him cringe every time we hit a bump in the road, but I assure him I am fine.

As the car pulls into our driveway I let out a sigh of relief. Walking into the house, I am greeted by my boys and Dan's parents. The house smells great. My sweet friend and bible study mate, Anne-Marie, has dropped off a pot roast dinner and Mom is heating the food while setting the table for dinner. The aroma of food is tempting, but my stomach is still a little weak. I nibble a few bites of the delicious food but mostly enjoy sitting at the table with my family. The boys fill me in the last few days' events – school, the hockey banquet and their silly antics. As the meal ends, Mom starts to clean up and Dad mentions I look exhausted. He leads me into the den where Mom has transformed the couch into a makeshift bed. I will sleep here for a few nights as it allows me to keep my head propped up and is much easier than lying flat.

Dan reviews all the paperwork regarding my restrictions and post-surgical care. He reminds me it's time for my pain medication and that later he will have to empty my drains. The drains will need to be emptied twice a day and measured. We need to keep a daily record of the amount of fluid to report to the doctor before our next visit.

Following Mom and Dad's departure, the boys and Dan join me in the den to watch TV. Drowsy, but content to have all my men around me, I can finally rest. I know I will sleep well tonight because I am home. At approximately 9 p.m., the phone rings and it is Dr. Dapper checking to make sure I am fine. Dan speaks with him, clarifies a few things he is concerned with regarding my care, thanks him and hangs up. About a half an hour later, my breast surgeon calls. She tells Dan she has good news. She rushed the pathology of my lymph nodes and the lab found no sign of growth or cancer. I can continue with immediate reconstruction and require no radiation. Praise God! Two days ago, I had a bilateral mastectomy, eight lymph nodes removed and expanders put in to start immediate reconstruction. Nevertheless, I am slowly being rebuilt and I'm officially heading down the road to recovery.

Chapter 12

God Cares

Recovery requires me to make a mental mind shift, as I am not dealing well with all the restrictions. My post surgical instructions include no heavy lifting, no strenuous activity and no vigorous exercise. I have plastic tubes with drains extending from my body collecting fluid and I am taking opioids for pain. This presents a problem for me, the "über task master," but it is also a huge lesson God is teaching me. One of the conclusions I come to is that God did not bring me through all of this so that I can live another day just to dust or vacuum or straighten up my house. He brought me through this experience to teach me what is important. Enjoy life. Cherish my family and friends and spend time with them. Don't sweat the small stuff. Find something positive in everything. Slowly I am learning how to let go. Feeling vulnerable makes me pare down my concerns in life and to confront what's really important and relinquish the things that aren't.

That evening it is all reinforced when John and Daniel gingerly kiss me good night and tell me they are glad I am okay. I tell them I am sorry to have missed their hockey banquet. Now, with hockey over, lacrosse season is just beginning and I apologize in advance for not being able to make some of their upcoming games. I start to get upset. I have been their room mom, team mom and carpool mom. It disappoints me to not be at their games. They look at me tenderly, John with his warm brown eyes and Daniel with his baby blues. Daniel rubs my back and John kisses my head. At the same time they say, "Mom, we just want you here!" Through the love of my beautiful boys, I realize my daily tasks can be completed by anyone if need be. It's not what I do but who I am that is irreplaceable. I think we all sleep well that night. I start the next day resting in God's care, which comes through His people in many ways. Some say it takes a village. I say it takes a church. What it really takes are the people that God uses to deliver His care.

JP visits the next day with a selection of hair bands because she knows I am stressing about my hair during my "no shower" restriction. She tells Dan and me she has been overwhelmed with emails from friends. She shares with us that the moms in my bible study and church have set up a schedule to provide meals for my family. What a beautiful expression of love and caring. She also tells us that she has an army of people at the ready offering to clean, wash, sweep, wipe counters and anything else I may need. This helps me understand why God says to us in *Psalm 46:10: Be still and know that I am God.* It is one I meditated on many times during procedures and surgeries, but also one that I need on a daily basis before I jump into each day. Maybe in addition to being silent so that I hear the whispers of God, I need to be still to see Him at work.

I sleep most of the weekend, but am humbled by the many times the doorbell rings with deliveries of flowers, candy and fruit. Dan takes off from work to be with me as I heal and drives me to my upcoming doctor visits during the week.

During the next few visits to the doctor, my drains are removed, my dressings are changed and I am fitted into a surgical bra. It's white and cotton and reminds me of those ugly nursing bras. With each passing visit this week, I fill in my goal sheet, a spreadsheet I made before the mastectomy, starting with the date of surgery and ending approximately five months later. It includes an area to track my medications, fluid volumes while the drains are in place and a calendar to schedule doctor visits and major events. My goal is to get back and make all these activities: lacrosse games for the boys, John's prom and high school graduation and my high school reunion picnic. The schedule also notes the upcoming trip to Aruba in early August, and college "moving in" day for John in late August.

I am now ready for my first expansion visit. Tissue expansion is a process that stretches your remaining chest skin and soft tissues to make room for the breast implant. Breast reconstruction begins with placement of a tissue expander and often requires multiple "fill-ups" before the space in the chest is ready for an implant. JP not only drives me to my appointment, but is also brave enough to come into the room with me as I get "inflated." Now that's a great friend! As I sit on the exam table and watch as the surgeon and nurse start to fill the expanders in my chest, I chuckle at how absurd this must look. He uses a magnet to locate a small valve in each expander and inserts a needle. I flinch a little from the pinch of the needle. He says that is a good sign as I still have some feeling in that area. The doctor and nurse each hold a syringe filled with saline. Slowly they push the liquid through the valve that leads to the open space in the expander. I feel a little pressure as the tissue starts to stretch. JP almost falls over when I ask the surgeon when I can start to vacuum again. (Okay, I know I vowed to let go of the obsessive cleaning, but change takes time!) He looks at her and then at me and confesses he has never been asked that question. He says I should think of other things to do like gardening or fine dining. After the poison sumac incident I think I would rather use my Dyson! By the time JP drops me off at home, I am tired and uncomfortable from the effects of the stretching. My back muscles seem to be screaming. I take some medicine and try to sleep.

My schedule starts to lose its prominence during the expansion process. I refer to my planner less and less as my recovery starts going off track. After a day out with Mom, about two weeks post surgery, my left hand swells up and causes numbness in my arm. I call the doctor. I have lymphedema, which is a side effect that can happen as a result of the removal of the lymph nodes. Lymphedema can also result from blockages in the lymphatic system, one that runs closely with the circulatory system to return fluid from tissues. It essentially acts like a filter for toxins and cells such as cancer. The nurse encourages me to try and manage it by massaging my arm with upward strokes and keeping it elevated as much as possible. She coaxes me to rest and tells me the doctor wants me to make an appointment with the physical therapy department. In addition to the swollen left arm, I notice some redness at the incision line on my right breast. I am due for another expansion in a few days so I wait until I get to the office to show the doctor.

As I sit on the exam table, I open my dressing gown and point out the redness before the doctor locates the valve in the tissue expander. He gently inspects the area and says, "Let's make an appointment for first thing Monday morning. We will not be doing any expansion today. I need to relieve the pressure on the right side as there may be an infection in that area." He then proceeds to withdraw the saline in the right expander. I watch as it deflates and feel my spirits deflate as well.

Outside of the exam room, the scheduler tells me to report back to the hospital at 5 a.m. Monday – the day before my twentieth wedding anniversary. I am devastated at the realization I need another surgery.

The pain is excruciating and I become consumed with thoughts of another surgery, new healing times and possible drains again. A time of moving forward has just turned into a huge step backwards. Because each step in reconstruction needs a three-month window of healing, I quickly tick off the months and realize my plan to be done by August, ready and looking like a Baywatch lifeguard is over! Well, perhaps I was a little delusional in that goal anyway.

I sleep most of the weekend, partly because of the pain, and partly because I am emotionally and physically drained. I talk to a few close friends and family and tell them the latest news. My friend, Patti, after hearing my laments, chastises me by saying, "Barb, this wasn't a manicure you just had. Give yourself a break!" My step mom, Rose, ever patient and wise, tells me to take my concerns and let them go like a helium balloon up to God. A survivor of ovarian cancer herself, she recounts her journey and how she got through it all. She says she learned to listen to her body and although she had great support from my dad, she realized God was the one who had her life in His hands. Through it all – surgery and many rounds of chemotherapy – she always made it a point to be thankful and cheerful. I realize how blessed I am that I was spared chemotherapy and that I did not lose my hair. How dare I complain? My dad always says, "Things could always be worse," but I have mixed feelings about that. I am mad at myself for allowing all of these "pity parties." I try to relax a little and send my cares off in a balloon, but I still can't seem to get the dark clouds to pass just yet.

The dark clouds part the day after Palm Sunday. Since it is Easter week, I spend some time thinking about the passion of Christ – how He even asked for this cup to be taken away from Him, and yet, He trusted and did what He needed to do. These reflections help me tremendously. I am yet at another point of trusting and taking more steps. Steps I find difficult to take. I concentrate on God's goodness and faithfulness and recognize the need to change the way I am thinking about my current situation. I need not be so prideful to think I know how things should turn out. Maybe this surgery is the best thing. Maybe this set back will actually be helpful in my complete recovery.

Let God transform you into a new person by changing the way you think. Romans 12:2 NLT

One of the ways I change my way of thinking is to consider others and to pray for them. I am very fortunate to be able to communicate with so many people while I go through all of this. My sisters, knowing it would be hard for me to reach and lift my laptop, buy me an iPad. It is such a great gift and light enough for me to use to email friends as I convalesce. It allows me to continue to get the prayer request updates from my church. It is very important for me to continue to pray for others as it helps me turn my focus away from my own needs. Prayer is a privilege and a responsibility that I can do for others, especially right now when I can't do much else. I gain a better perspective which helps with my attitude. I remind myself He is in control.

The encouragement and support of my family and friends is tremendous. Every card I receive stands open on my dining room table and foyer console so I can read them. They give me an instant "pick me up" whenever I need it and remind me how loved I am and how kind people are. During times of hardship, I sometimes want to retreat and isolate myself. This time I humble myself to be open to others who just want to show me love.

On a particularly difficult day I find myself walking around the house aimlessly. I pick up one of the cards on the foyer console. It is from a woman from church whom I barely know. Enclosed in her card is a note sharing her experience with breast cancer and reconstruction years earlier. She includes her phone number and tells me to call anytime. I decide to take her up on her offer. Calling her is a huge help and I quickly make a new friend. Hearing her story and sharing mine helps me to relax a little more, humble myself and allow myself to heal, this time not just physically, but mentally as well. One day at a time.

The unexpected surgery to replace the expander and eliminate the excess fluid goes well. The nurses and doctor are wonderful and luckily I do not have to stay overnight, but can return home. Dan and I celebrate our twentieth anniversary together at home with the boys. It's better than any anniversary with flowers, a fancy, new dress or dining at a great restaurant. After twenty years, Dan and I are still side-by-side, still in love and living through our vows of sickness and health and better or worse moments. That is something to celebrate. In typical style, my sons and my husband make me laugh and smile and feel loved. I don't need anything else. Later that night, I give Dan his anniversary gift – a letter I wrote to him expressing my gratitude and love, and my hope for many more anniversaries to come. The next morning I see the letter tucked into his bible.

A few days later while recouping, Cat, my dear friend from high school, calls me to check in. Cat is one of those people who can be brutally honest with you no matter what, but makes you still feel loved at the same time. I confess to Cat that I've been feeling very down and recount the need for a second surgery to repair my right breast which resembled a deflated soufflé. In her usual quick wittedness Cat replies, "Hey, you know what they say? If the soufflé goes bad, call it a lava cake!" I start to laugh so hard that tears form and I realize they're happy tears and not tears of self-pity.

Another encouraging phone call comes from one of my favorite pastors. No longer serving at my church, Pastor Pete has always stayed in touch with my family. He, along with my current pastors, Bruce and Brad, are on the recipient list of my emails.

I have a sure bet that these men have never heard so much talk about breasts in their entire lives! Sometimes I doubt whether I should include them in my updates, but their guidance and counsel have always been important to me and I want them to know what I am going through. One afternoon Pastor Pete calls to check in on me. We chat for a while, he prays for us as a family and is thankful for being a part of our lives and sharing in how God has blessed us. As a husband and father of two girls, he tells me he is so thankful for my openness and sharing of my situation. He tells me my emails have allowed him to gain insight into this particular struggle and it has been helpful to him as he ministers to other women in similar situations. That makes me feel so good. I am glad I am a "communicator" if it allows me to help others.

I need to get to physical therapy to address the bout of lymphedema. The swelling is better, but the breast surgeon still wants me to go, especially since I had a little set back. The second surgery is delaying my post surgery exercise and my mobility is suffering. I have gotten stiffer and my muscles are getting more rigid. Every morning I wake up in pain. Before I get out of bed, I have to sit up and wait as a wave of pain takes over the area between my shoulder blades. I sit still and try to breathe, but sometimes the pain is so bad it takes my breath away. I try to sleep propped up but nothing is helping with my morning hour transition. The pain gets better during the day, but it is not pleasant at all. The opposing muscles in my back scream about the stretching that is going on in the front.

In May I finally start physical therapy and hope it will help combat the swelling, pain and stiffness. My therapist's name is Rita, which was my mom's name. She is an occupational therapist and she is wonderful! She is tall and lean and has a tender way about her. She helps me relax and gain confidence as I learn exercises to help with my mobility and strength. I need to overcome the fear that I will hurt or damage my upper body and end up with another surgery. She pushes me to challenge my rotations and extensions and lay in positions without fear of harm to the surgical site. She tends to my body and mind. Unintentionally, I have developed a habit of walking with my arms close to my body in a very protective stance. The exercises encourage me to stand tall and not shrink into the shadows afraid to be exposed or hurt again.

Around this time, a lovely couple in our church gives birth to a baby boy. We had been praying for them for quite some time as their sonogram revealed the baby would be born with spina bifida, a congenital disorder that affects the protective closure of the vertebrae around the spinal cord. When I receive the email announcement that he is born, I look at this sweet baby's picture and am able to raise my arms in praise to God for this beautiful new life. It means so much to perform this simple act of praise. Thank you Rita. Thank You God! This precious boy was born with spina bifida, but is strong enough to withstand the surgeries he needs the day after his birth. I look at the picture of him and his precious face and just know God has big, wonderful plans for him.

My prayer journal seems to have many requests for people who need healing. Prayer requests from church and friends include upcoming surgeries, past hurts, cancer and other struggles of life. Sometimes as I make a prayer list I feel overwhelmed, but there again lies the need to pray. I know my list is not overwhelming for God. He hears every prayer. For us, sometimes we don't see the healing we want on earth. I don't understand all that I see, the suffering that happens. However I rest in the faithfulness and promises of God. Can life be hard? Yes. Hopeless? Never if your hope is in Him.

When I don't attend church, I like to watch a bible ministry show on television. One Sunday morning in June, I am watching a favorite of mine, "In Touch Ministries" with Dr. Charles Stanley. His sermon focuses on healing and catches my attention. An important point he makes is that healing is a promise from God. God is the Great Physician. Doctors practice medicine, but God heals. He refers to *Jeremiah 30:17* which says *I will restore your health and will heal you of your wounds.* Dr. Stanley goes on to say that if all we need is physical healing, God would have sent a doctor, but His primary purpose is to be our Savior! Our healing goes far beyond this life and will allow us to live eternally with Him despite what our bodies may endure on earth.

Thankfully, as time goes on I heal physically and am able to enjoy many celebrations, including Daniel's fifteenth birthday, John's prom and his high school graduation and senior lacrosse day. Our plans for Aruba come true as well. I enjoy the precious time with my family and I can finally relax. I am cautious not to get burned since any damage to the thin skin on my chest could possibly delay the next procedure. Lathering on mounds of sunscreen, I carefully try to stay out of the sun and wear my new protective sun shirts and a wide rim hat. I return with great memories and the feeling that all is well again.

The final exchange surgery takes place two weeks after our return home. Some more healing is needed, but the recovery isn't bad and the implants feel more comfortable than the expanders. My arm no longer swells either! I opt for the exchange to be my last invasive step in the reconstruction process.

At the end of that same week, we move John into his college dorm, two hours away. Mom and Dad join us and we form a car caravan to Pennsylvania. As I see the state welcome sign, I start to tear up, believing my heart is about to break. Leaving your child at college can be very poignant and for me it just adds to the emotional rollercoaster I've been riding for the last few months. I think back to when John was a little boy and we spent our summer vacations at Hershey Park in "Wennsylwania" as he used to call it. Now, as I turn around, I see in the back seat of the car a fully-grown, handsome, capable eighteen-year-old, leaving home for the first time, ready to start a new chapter in his life. Next to him sits my baby, Daniel. I remind myself to cherish the next three years at home with Daniel before I have to take him to college and say goodbye.

Life moves on and there is so much to look forward to as my boys become men and Dan and I enter a new season.

> *I know the plans I have for you,* declares the *Lord,*
> *plans to prosper you and not to harm you, plans to*
> *give you hope and a future. Jeremiah 29:11*

Chapter 13

This is the Day the Lord has Made

It's September and a new routine is in place. Now it is just Daniel and I at home in the mornings before school. Even though I miss John, I enjoy my special time devoted completely to my youngest. As I make him breakfast, we chat and then I drive him to school each day. Afterward, I stop at Panera's for my usual morning coffee before going to the gym.

Next month is Breast Cancer Awareness so I decide to email my gal pals to "get their pink on." I am almost done with reconstruction and want to celebrate. I plan a luncheon with all my friends who have been there with me through all of this and want them to promise me to take care of their "gals!" I am also looking forward to getting them all in a room together. So many of them have chatted over email these past two years, but have never met. All my friends cannot wait to meet JP whose wit and savvy communication kept them abreast of my situation since March. I love my friends and cherish each and every one's impact on my life. They are all different, but each fulfills such a special part of me. Cat sends a gift from Vegas despite not being able to attend. It's a pink tee shirt that says, "Yes, these are fake. My real ones tried to kill me!" Seven months after the mastectomy, although not all done, we are going to celebrate! I am happy with my new breasts because they no longer pose a threat to my survival. It is time to rejoice with the women who have encouraged me, prayed for me, helped me and cried with me. We start our lunch with a prayer of thanks and praise to God. Of course I shed a few tears, but all in all, it is a very joyful day.

My body is almost back to normal. I still have dark purple lines across each breast mound, reminding me where I was cut. I make the decision to forfeit the nipple reconstruction as it requires a skin graft and in my mind it is not necessary. In its place, I decide to schedule 3-D nipple tattoos on my chest. This type of tattooing is a great alternative to nipple/areola reconstruction, giving the illusion of a raised nipple without additional surgery. I make the appointment to do it right before Christmas. I really want to be done with everything before the year ends. I want to put the past two years behind me and look forward to the New Year.

For me, the tattooing represents a final touch and a completion of God's work on my body over the past few years and time to move on. Four days before Christmas 2012, my plastic surgeon uses his artistic abilities to complete my reconstruction. I am awake through the entire process; we chat about the upcoming holidays and before I know it, I am done!

For a fleeting moment, I actually consider getting another tattoo somewhere else on my body with a favorite verse, but in the end, decide my scars are enough of a physical reminder of how God heals.

Thankfully, I can start wearing regular bras again. I buy a few options based on the doctor's suggestions and bring them in to my next visit to get fitted. Some women say it is unnecessary to wear a bra after reconstruction; however, my surgeon recommends I do. I have a little anxiety over the fit, adjusting to the newness. Despite being assured there is nothing to fear, the underwire is unnerving so I opt out of those.

While sorting through my clothes to get rid of what doesn't fit anymore, I discover a whole drawer full of "special" bras that are now going in the trash. Some I have had for years and barely wore while others remain unworn and still have the tags on them. I start to think about all the things I put away for special occasions and then never use. Clothes and bras, china, jewelry; these are not treasures to be stored up. What was I waiting for? Why is it my life tends to revolve around a perpetual affinity for tomorrow? Fortunately, facing the threat of breast cancer has taught me a valuable lesson. Stop saving things for another time. Stop imagining a better day or a better place to wear the things you love. Enjoy them, use them, and instead of waiting for a "special day," realize it is here and now.

> *Matthew 6:19-21: Do not lay up for yourselves treasures on earth, where moth and rust destroy and where thieves break in and steal, but lay up for yourselves treasures in heaven, where neither moth nor rust destroys and where thieves do not*

break in and steal. For where your treasure is,
there your heart will be also.

In the same respect, I learn that exquisite china, fancy table settings and a perfect house are not the recipe for a happy home. This was never more apparent to me than four days after Dan's accident when he finally returned home from the hospital. We were home celebrating a belated Thanksgiving with all of our extended family. I knew there was much to thank God for and the realization that every day should be a day of thanks crossed my mind. That weekend, with all the family together, we ate on paper plates in the den with joyful hearts. What truly mattered was the love that permeated the room. It was easily the best day we spent in a long time. Emmanuel, God is with us!

Psalm 118:24 ESV: This is the day that the Lord
has made; let us rejoice and be glad in it.

There is always something to be thankful for and a reason to praise God. We are told not to complain because when we do we are not trusting God in the situation. This has helped me change my perspective on things in many ways. I remind myself of some of the reasons to be thankful. I am healthy again and I have my wonderful family. My perspective on housework has changed. I may need to do tasks for my family, but these necessities are not my identity. My family doesn't love me because I do things for them. They appreciate what I do for them because they know I do it out of love for them. I don't earn love by performance. What a great parallel to God's unconditional love and grace towards us. Full disclosure – I still have my cranky days and I need to rest at times to refresh my mood, but in general I can keep those emotions in check and make a real effort to see the glass half full and sometimes half full can lead to a cup runneth over. Positively taking stock in our circumstances can really turn the tide of our emotions. For me it is the realization that, although I have new scars and a different body, I am healing, healthy and moving forward. I am also coming to the end of a trial and venturing into a new season of my life with a hopeful heart.

Ecclesiastes 3:1-8 ESV

For everything there is a season, and a time for every matter under heaven:

A time to be born, and a time to die;
A time to plant, and a time to pluck up what is planted;
A time to kill, and a time to heal;
A time to break down, and a time to build up;
A time to weep, and a time to laugh;
A time to mourn, and a time to dance;
A time to cast away stones, and a time to gather stones together;
A time to embrace, and a time to refrain from embracing;
A time to seek, and a time to lose;
A time to keep, and a time to cast away;
A time to tear, and a time to sew;
A time to keep silence, and a time to speak;
A time to love, and a time to hate;
A time for war, and a time for peace.

As December comes to a close, I happen upon *Luke 4:38-39,* a verse that I find meaningful to my yearlong journey: *And He arose and left the synagogue and entered Simon's house. Now Simon's mother-in-law was ill with a high fever, and they appealed to Him on her behalf. And He stood over her and rebuked the fever, and it left her, and immediately she rose and began to serve them.*

I am especially taken by how Simon's mother-in-law was healed and immediately started serving. I know Jesus healed me. Now I need to continue to serve. Isn't that what life is all about? I am not always sure what my service will look like, but I know if I love and continue to look to the needs of others, I will find my way. If we use the resources and talents God has given us, I think we have a good head start to various ministries. Some of the ones that draw me in right now are the continuing leadership in the bible study I do with the moms from the preschool, as well as a meal ministry in my church. I just need to keep my eyes and heart open and look to Him for His guidance.

Chapter 14

Look Ahead, Look Up

S ummer 2013: I am at the breast center once again. This time I feel free. I am renewed. Here for my first yearly checkup with the breast surgeon, I am ready to hear some good news for a change. Although my initial meeting with her more than a year ago was positive, I carried some heavy concerns in my mind and in my heart and was confused about choices available to me at that time.

Sometimes our decisions are just one of many alternate routes we can take, and without God's wisdom, we may later second-guess ourselves. Today I feel blessed with God's direction throughout the last two years. As the surgeon reviews my post surgical pathology report, she shakes her head and reminds me of the findings – pervasiveness ALH in both breasts. She seems very certain it was inevitable that cancer would have developed. Looking at me, she says, "Thank God, we did the right thing." Thank God is right! I truly believe the wisdom and strength I received suspended the inevitable development of breast cancer. I leave the office with no other instructions than a note to call next year for a check up.

My husband, sons, family and friends now think of the past few years as just a faint memory. For me, most of my memories like my scars have not faded one hundred percent. They remain clear and vivid to this day and I cherish them for they remind me of my intimacy with God, the confidence that He always hears my prayers and the peace and joy that are mine when I meditate on His word. Beautiful times! In the fervor of jumping back into life, I have days where I need to remind myself why I am here. What gets me through the day? What grounds me when I have bad days? What guides me through life? I try to remain grateful in all circumstances and praise Him every day. I want to remain at peace, rest in Him, trust in Him and know that He is in control. My experience has strengthened my trust in God and defined my beliefs in Him and how I look at life.

When I meet women who are experiencing a similar struggle, or talk to a friend who knows someone who has breast cancer, my heart goes out to them and I pray they will have the support, confidence and peace they need to completely heal.

Recently, at a lacrosse tournament at Boston University, I meet a woman who I believe I was destined to connect with. Overhearing Dan and I discuss the fact that we forgot to pack Daniel's shorts, she kindly offers to lend us a pair of her son's. Gratefully, Daniel takes the shorts and runs off to join his team, leaving us to walk to the bleachers together. We start to talk and during our conversation she shares with me that she has two sons and has been struggling with multiple biopsies and breast issues. God is showing me that in the same way many women have shared their stories with me, I too have a story to share.

After I recount my journey and we discuss her concerns, she tells me that she believes we were destined to meet. I agree and feel good knowing in some way my story may have helped her. Though a complete stranger, at the end of the game we hugged each other and I promised to pray for her and the difficult decisions she would soon have to make. I believe God puts people together for a reason. Maybe it is for us to learn something from each other or to encourage each other in times of uncertainty or stress.

December 2013: A milestone for me. One year since my last procedure. Life is slowly returning to normal – my "new normal" as I call it. I feel more like "me" and don't identify myself as a "patient" anymore. I am aware of the implants at times and a constant tightness in my chest, and then there are times I can't remember not having these silicone mounds. My stamina has increased, I am back on a routine at the gym, I lead bible study on a regular basis, work, do my "mom thing" and enjoy the new milestones for my son Daniel – his driving permit, selecting colleges, lacrosse games and so much more.

One very important part of my recovery process is exercise. When I did the Daniel Fast, I learned that I am composed of a physical body, a soul which is the center of emotional/fleshly desire, and the Spirit, the indwelling of the Holy Spirit. The fast helped me to control my soul and teach me to focus on being led by the Spirit, but I still need to care for my physical body as best I can. The care of my body enables me to serve my family and others and to regain the stamina and physical strength I lost during the surgeries. In addition to cardio and weight training, I attend a yoga class. The stretching is tremendous as it helps with circulation and nerves. Some of the positions are similar to what Rita taught me in physical therapy. As a Christian, my meditation time is focused on personal prayers and sometimes I recite one of my favorites, the prayer of St. Francis. Some of the yoga positions refer to eagles or looking out over a cliff. When I do these positions, I think of the trust I have in God and how I want it to grow. My favorite verse during the eagle position is *Isaiah 40:31 (NIV): But those who hope in the Lord will renew their strength. They will soar on wings like eagles; they will run and not grow weary, they will walk and not be faint.* I continue to renew my strength, both physically and spiritually.

At the end of each yoga class, the instructor asks the class to take a bow to our higher self. I know I only have a higher self when the Spirit of Christ leads me. When asked to do this, I raise my hand and take a bow to the one who saves me, Jesus Christ. That gives me peace or "Namaste" as they say.

One day after a class, I ask the trainer for advice about some moves to adapt to the way my body feels post surgery. I share my story. She looks at me and says, "Wow, you are an overcomer!" I leave the gym, hop in the car, buckle up and turn on the radio, listening as I drive away. I start to sing along, realizing it's one of my favorite songs, "Overcomer" by Mandisa. "You're an overcomer, stay in the fight 'til the final round. You're not going under, 'cause God is holding you right now ..." I sing at the top of my lungs and think how God is with me, how He holds me and how I am indeed an overcomer!

As life goes on, I reflect on a situation I never would have wished for and prayed would not happen, yet now I stand here and thank God for it. What is so good about having a double mastectomy at the age of forty-six? Well, for one thing my diagnosis changed everything, especially what I know about myself. I learned that every day is a good day, some better than others. I learned that I am surrounded by people that are good, I mean really good. I learned to live life with a greater sense of urgency. I learned that I can be strong and spirited and yet vulnerable and fragile. Most important, I learned that God is always with me. I thank God for the walk with Him, for the times He carried me, for my spiritual progress and growth, and for the blessings of having a relationship with Him. I look to the future prayerfully trusting in God's promises. Daily I need to read his Word, remind myself when I stray and look for ways to share the good news with others. I am so grateful to be alive and serving Him.

March 7, 2014 – My Facebook post for the day:

Two years ago today, by the grace of God, I gave breast cancer the big ol' raspberry! I almost forgot this anniversary, which means I have been blessed to heal and move on. Yet I will always remember God's goodness and faithfulness to me along the way. I have not forgotten all the people He showered on me to deliver my care. So to all of you I say, "Thank you and I love you." Every prayer, card, call, text, post, visit, "cheer up" gift, meal and more, strengthened and helped restore me. My family and I are ever grateful.

Lamentations 3:22-24: The Lord's loving kind-nesses indeed never cease, for His compassions never fail. They are new every morning; great is your faithfulness. The Lord is my portion, says my soul, therefore I have hope in Him.

Genesis 26:24b: ... Do not be afraid for I am with you ...

Psalm 27:1: The Lord is my light and my salvation – whom shall I fear? The Lord is the stronghold of my life – of whom shall I be afraid?

Epilogue

I may not end up meeting you, the reader, but I hope I do. If not, I pray in some small way I have given you encouragement for your journey in life, a desire to find your walk with God and seek Him so you may find the wisdom you need in life. I invite you to:

- **Get to know God** – *Jesus answered, I am the way and the truth and the life. No one comes to the Father except through me. John 14:6 NIV*

- **Read God's Word** – *Every word of God is flawless; He is a shield to those who take refuge in him. Proverbs 30:5 NIV*

- **Trust God** – *Trust in the LORD with all your heart and lean not on your own understanding; in all your ways submit to him, and he will make your paths straight. Proverbs 3:5-6 NIV*

- **Pray** – *Rejoice always, pray continually, give thanks in all circumstances; for this is God's will for you in Christ Jesus. 1 Thessalonians 5:16-18* NIV

- **Be part of a community of believers** – *Therefore encourage one another and build each other up, just as in fact you are doing. 1 Thessalonians 5:11* NIV

- **Embrace each day** – *This is the day that the Lord has made; let us rejoice and be glad in it. Psalm 118:24*

- **Take knowledge from the past and look to the future with hope** – *The steadfast love of the* LORD *never ceases; His mercies never come to an end; they are new every morning; great is your faithfulness. The* LORD *is my portion, says my soul, therefore I will hope in Him. Lamentations 3:22-24* ESV

- **Know that God loves you** – *For God so loved the world, that He gave his only Son, that whoever believes in Him should not perish but have eternal life. John 3:16* ESV

- **Love yourself, let others love you and love them back** – *Love is patient and kind; love does not envy or boast; it is not arrogant or rude. It does not insist on its own way; it is not irritable or resentful; it does not rejoice at wrongdoing, but* *rejoices with the truth. Love bears all things, believes all things, hopes all things, endures all things. Love never ends. As for prophecies, they will pass away; as for tongues, they will cease; as for knowledge, it will pass away. For we know in part and we prophesy in part, but when the perfect comes, the partial will pass away. When I was a child, I spoke like a child; I thought like a child, I reasoned like a child. When I became a man, I gave up childish ways. For now we see in a mirror dimly, but then face to face. Now I know in part; then I shall know fully, even as I have been fully known. So now faith, hope, and love abide, these three; but the greatest of these is love. 1 Corinthians 13:4-14 ESV*

Do not forsake wisdom, and she will protect you;
love her, and she will watch over you.
Proverbs 4:6 NIV

Acknowledgements

Although much of my story is about my relationship with God, I am grateful for the many people He provided to help me through my journey. Their prayers, encouragement, physical support, love, basic provisions and kindness were and are a huge blessing in my life.

To Dan, my wonderful husband of twenty-two years, God truly "blessed the broken road that led me straight to you." You intuitively always know my feelings and when you reassured me with those simple words, "You know, no matter what this is, we are going to get through this" I was truly uplifted. You are and will always be by my side and because of this I can do anything. You are the most amazing blessing God has given me and I thank you for loving me so much!

To my sons, John and Daniel – when a mother is pregnant, the beating of her heart is necessary to keep her baby alive. Since your births, your beating hearts are what keep me alive. This surgery was done for my future, the future that includes you and your families. I am honored to be your mom and my happiness lies in watching how you live your lives. I pray you grow closer to God every day.

To my wonderful mother-in-law, Renee, who was there each day serving my every need and sharing my highs, lows, complaints, frustrations and joys. You drove me to office visits, shopped for bras with me, cared for my every whim and those of my family. I can't even count the amount of laundry and dishes you washed. Thank you for raising my wonderful husband and always treating me like a daughter. I love you!

And to the countless other family and friends, my dad Bob and step mom Rose, father-in-law John, sisters Carolyn and Jennifer, my sisters in Christ and my email bunch who faithfully read the updates and prayed for me – JP (communicator extraordinaire), Pat M., Deirdre, Debbie, Linda, Suzanne, Courtney, Helen K., Carol, Elaine, Helen O., Lenny, Miriam, Michele, Laura, Joanne, Lecia, Kristina, Anne-Marie, Cathy

H., Cathy L., Maria, and Pat B.), Hillside Church and my wonderful pastors Bruce, Brad and Pete, Roxbury Community Bible Study ladies, my phenomenal doctors – Julie DiGioia MD, Elissa Santoro MD and Scott Spiro MD, all the medical personnel and staff at Overlook Hospital and St. Barnabas Medical Center, fellow Christians I have never met (but will someday) such as the ladies at Ledgewood Baptist who knitted me a prayer shawl, Star 99.1 radio, my Harvesting Hope families and my Facebook friends, especially my alumni from the St. Francis Prep Class of 1983, and Mikey P. – thank you for wearing your pink socks when you played lacrosse with John. Every card, note, phone call, visit, gift, meal, gesture of help, prayer and love are all treasured memories and blessings. You are all angels in my eyes and heart, as you truly are messengers of God who bring me comfort and the Good News!

Lastly and lovingly, to my dear Helen O. — I could not have gotten through the re-reads and editing process without you! You have always had a gift of getting the thoughts out of my head and on paper. Thank you for allowing me to relive my emotions, helping me to laugh and cry all over again and for encouraging me to share my blessings with the reader. Thank you, thank you, thank you!

Reflection/Discussion Questions

1. What is the significance of prayer in your life?

2. How has prayer helped to guide you in making the right decisions?

3. In addition to prayer, how do you share your feelings with God?

4. What is the difference between knowledge and wisdom? How do you attain knowledge? How do you attain wisdom?

5. What does God's will mean to you and how does it affect the way you live your life?

6. Do your emotions always align with your faith? Do you think we have to make a choice to act a certain way despite our feelings?

7. Have you ever encountered a frightening situation similar to what happened in the book? How did you respond to it?

8. How do you make each day special for you and your family?

9. Were there any particular bible verses in this book that had special meaning for you and if so, why?

10. How does God's word affect how you view life? How does it affect your prayer life? How does it affect how you look at the future?

11. How can you develop a better understanding of God's word?

12. Do you have people in your life with whom you can communicate and reach out to for support?

13. What are some ways you feel God's special presence in your life?

14. Have you ever processed the thought of dying? How did it make you feel?

15. Have any of your views or thoughts changed after reading this book?

Suggested Readings:

The Holy Bible – any version

"The Yada Yada Prayer Group Series" by Neta Jackson

"The Bible Jesus Read" by Philip Yancey

"One Year Alone with God" by Ava Pennington

"The Daniel Fast" by Susan Gregory

"Captivating" by Jon and Stasi Eldridge

Additional Resources:

Dr. Charles Stanley – In Touch Ministries www.intouch.org

Take Them a Meal www.takethemameal.com

The Breast Reconstruction Guidebook, Second Edition by Kathy Steligo

Little Pink Houses of Hope www.littepink.org

Facing Our Risk of Cancer Empowered (FORCE)

www.facingourrisk.org

www.cancer.gov/cancertopics/factsheet/Risk/BRCA

About The Author

Barb is currently living in NJ with her princes - Dan, John and Daniel. John is doing great in college and Daniel is starting to look at schools. Barb trusts in the plans she knows God has for all of them and hopes they include a log cabin on a lake for retirement.

CPSIA information can be obtained at www.ICGtesting.com
Printed in the USA
LVOW10s1047180614

390605LV00003B/90/P